PELICAN BOOKS

A881

SEX AND THE SIGNIFICANT AMERICANS

John F. Cuber is Professor of Sociology at Ohio State University and has had twenty-five years of extensive experience in marriage counseling and related research. He is the author of several books and articles; his text, *Sociology: A Synopsis of Principles,* has sold over a quarter of a million copies. Peggy B. Harroff is a sociologist and has worked with Doctor Cuber on a number of his research projects.

SEX AND THE

SIGNIFICANT AMERICANS

*A Study of Sexual Behavior
Among the Affluent*

BY JOHN F. CUBER
WITH
PEGGY B. HARROFF

PENGUIN BOOKS
BALTIMORE • MARYLAND

Penguin Books Inc
7110 Ambassador Rd., Baltimore, Md. 21207

This edition first published 1966 by arrangement with
Appleton-Century, New York

Reprinted 1968, 1969

SBN 14 020881 X

Printed in the United States of America

FOREWORD

EACH age has its own style of knowing or seeking to know the truth. For some, the larger laws of the world have been approachable only through divine revelation; for others, by means of the symbolism of epic stories and mythical heroes; for still others, via deductive reasoning from a priori premises.

Although our own era has more than one cognitive style, the one which most nearly dominates it is the statistical. In an age of uncertainties, we seek certainty in probability theory, averages, and extrapolations, and since this has succeeded brilliantly in the physical sciences, we have eagerly applied it to the study of human behavior. All the achievements of psychology and psychoanalysis still do not enable us to predict with any degree of certainty what any given individual will do in the future; it is therefore reassuring to ignore the individual and to deal with mankind en masse, like an aggregation of molecules, and to seek the socio-psychological equivalents of Boyle's Law and Charles's Law—that is, to sum up a host of bits of information on human behavior in the form of bell and bimodal curves, factor analyses, orthogonal rotations, and chi-square calculations.

All this has a satisfyingly scientific look, both because of the mathematical apparatus involved and the exactitude of the results obtained. And no doubt much real knowledge of human behavior has been obtained through this approach. One cannot be absolutely sure, for instance, whether adultery is a deviant form of behavior in our society or a normal one, until he knows what percentage of the population commits adultery and how often—and then goes on to correlate this activity with educational level, income, social status, and the like, to see whether it is deviant or normal for each social class.

Yet having learned all this, the social scientist has reached the limits of the quantitative method without learning the most important thing of all—how it feels to be an adulterer in our society. For the statistical method conveys nothing of the inner experiences that impel a man or woman to be unfaithful, and tells us nothing about whether the adulterous episodes themselves are trivial or profound, tawdry or poetic, innocuous or traumatic. The statistical method enables us to predict how most people in any specified group will probably behave, but not to describe how any of them actually feels; it leads only to a limited kind of knowledge— all denotation and no connotation.

And therefore it runs the risk of leading not to truth but to falsehood. The first Kinsey report taught us, for instance, that the average male reaches the peak of his sexual powers at the age of seventeen, and declines from then to the grave. Yet this fact rests upon computations of "frequency of outlet"—a series of statistics based on the assumption that all orgasms are to be counted as equal. Yet it is obvious that the emotional and spiritual meaning of an ejaculation achieved in two minutes by a masturbating seventeen-year-old is quite incommensurable with that of an ejaculation achieved by a mature male spending half an hour in bed with the woman he loves. Almost equally unhelpful are all those surveys of modern marriage which offer percentages in such categories as "very happy," "moderately happy," "somewhat unhappy," and so on, correlating these with income and other factors. One has only to recall the essayist William Hazlitt, whose years were filled with domestic discord, unrequited love, financial trouble, and ill health, and who, as he lay dying, seriously stated, "Well, I've had a happy life." If that statement were to become part of a statistic, we could be completely misled—though we never could be by an examination of Hazlitt's life.

It is refreshing, therefore, to find John F. Cuber and Peggy B. Harroff daring to swim against the mainstream of present-day social science in *The Significant Americans* and employing a wholly different cognitive style in their search for the truth about the sexual and emotional relationships between men and women of the upper middle class. Dr. Cuber and Mrs. Harroff wanted to find out how these people feel about premarital sex, married love, and extramarital relationships, and what part the male-female relationship plays in the success-oriented person's scheme of things—and they wanted to know all this not in terms of percentages but in terms of how it actually feels and looks to the persons involved.

The Significant Americans contains hundreds of direct quotations from its interviewees, plus some intriguing generalizations and patterns suggested by its authors; what it does not contain are tables, graphs, and calculations of statistical significance. One cannot find in it computations of orgasm frequency, or the percentage of unfaithful husbands and wives by five-year age groupings; what one can find, however, is how upper-middle-class people actually live and feel. It is the 1965 equivalent of a Pepys' *Diary* or a Rousseau's *Confessions*—a series of intimate revelations as seen and interpreted by competent trained behavioral scientists.

Dr. Cuber and Mrs. Harroff have written a book that is, perhaps, *sui generis:* it is something akin to descriptive anthropology but takes twentieth-century man as the "native"; it blends the individual case-reporting method of the psychotherapist with the sociologist's effort to see external patterns and regularities; it proceeds by intuition and perceptiveness rather than by mathematical rigor, but convinces us by force of its realism and insight. The methodologists will carp at it on any one of a score of grounds, but in the end we will have forgotten their decimal points and remembered the living persons we met, and understood, in the pages of this book. *The Significant Americans* is a significant contribution to the study of human love and marriage.

MORTON M. HUNT

AUTHORS' NOTE

"A MARRIED couple always presents an absurdly untruthful picture to the world," begins one of John O'Hara's soliloquies, "but it is a picture that the world finds convenient and a comfort. A couple are a man and a woman and what goes on between them the world never knows, could not possibly know. . . ." Yet the fiction writer does tell us what goes on between a man and a woman, often with arresting vividness. But he does so under the cloak of fiction. Even if he has carefully researched his subject and faithfully presented a social history, the writer of fiction can escape the cry "scandalmonger" or "exposé" because his readers need never quite face the pervasive realism implicit in the portrayal. The wholeness of the portrait and the insight of the artist can be dismissed as literary fiction. And so we still need to bring some manifest truth to the "absurd picture."

We present this report as a needed step in the direction of a synthesis of the wholeness and heart of the literary por-

trayal and the precision and objectivity of the scientific quest
for repetitive patterns of behavior. We have no cloak to pro-
tect us, or to lend to the reader. We cannot offer him the
escape that uncomfortable images are unique and dramatic
when they are widespread and ordinary. Nor can we claim
that the more startling characters in this book resemble real
people only through coincidence. Nor do we have the artist's
license to exaggerate the prosaic for dramatic effect. Both the
startling and the prosaic which our inquiries reveal are factually based upon long and intimate conversations with over
four hundred mature men and women. Whatever authen-
ticity it has is based on the realities of these people's lives.

While this study has been done exclusively by two people,
working closely together over a number of years, there is
acknowledged indebtedness to many others. An adequate list
of names would be as tedious as it would be honest. We therefore limit our acknowledgments to those who helped specif-
ically in the crystallization of ideas and in the final drafting
of the book: Mr. Jack Burton of Appleton-Century-Crofts,
Mr. Sidney Katz of the *Toronto Star* and Mr. Robert Levin
of *Redbook* magazine. We are most indebted, however, to the
people who provided the substance for the inquiry, the 437
distinguished Americans who, despite abundant justification
for pleading "too busy," gave generously of time and sometimes of hurtful memory. To these the book is rightfully
dedicated.

Walden Pond   J. F. C.
Galena, Ohio   P. B. H.

CONTENTS

THE
SIGNIFICANT
AMERICANS

Chapter 1

THE INQUIRY

THERE is continuing preoccupation in the professional literature on men and women, sex and marriage, with people caught in crises—divorce, immorality, or some psychological difficulties which have come to public or to clinical attention. Meanwhile, the great majority of people somehow manage to handle their intimate relations and cope with whatever difficulties arise without direct professional help. This large group has been virtually ignored in formal studies, even though it contains many sophisticated, educated, and otherwise knowledgeable people. To obtain a more accurate and better balanced picture of the male-female world, then, it seemed plausible to us to look to people who were apparently self-directed, not failures in any reasonable sense of the word. We wanted people who were also "normal" in the sense that they had not received clinical help for whatever problems they may have had. From such a group of adults, we hoped to learn some basic principles which researchers, who had focused directly on pathology, may have missed.

Although not our original intention, as it worked out, we soon found ourselves also with a more restricted, second focus: the influence of public success on the private life. A long-standing debate exists regarding such a connection. We are told, on the one hand, that success is generic, that people who are successful in one part of their lives are strongly inclined to be successful in other parts too. But we are also told that there is a contradiction between the public and the private phases, that people must choose between career dedication and personal fulfillment. Fame and fortune are said, in this view, to be bought at the price of a richer private life: one must make a choice, consciously or otherwise, to sacrifice or at least compromise in one aspect of life in order to achieve elsewhere. One man may want a close and central relationship with his wife and children more than he wants outstanding professional success, money, acclaim, power, or any of the other things by which a man is measured these days. And so he fashions a modest blueprint for his professional life. Another may reason that the measure of a man lies in career achievement and if this calls for sacrifice or atrophy of the private side of life, he considers it either as inevitable or as worth the price. But all this, however plausible, is speculative; perhaps when we take a look at real people and their life circumstances, we may come closer to knowing how the public and private spheres are related.

The Significant Americans

The people we chose for study are a roughly representative group of the leadership echelon, the decision-making, policy-forming people, the most clearly successful, as success is currently conceived. In other investigations people like them have been designated Elites, Eminents, Top Influentials, and more academically, Upper Middle Class. They are among the most highly educated and are the models of achievement to which the ambitious aspire. They are socially conspicuous, not necessarily by choice but because the nature of their work in the independent professions, government, the arts, commerce, and the military keeps them collectively and individually in the public eye. They are, almost any way one cares to look at them, *Significant* Americans.

Interviewees, by Sex and Occupation

	Men	Women	Total
Artists (10)	9	1	10
Business Executives: (81)			
"Organization" men and women	36	9	45
"Small business" owners or top managers	27	9	36
Clergymen (17)	17	0	17
Government Officials: (55)			
Appointed	17	12	29
Elected	23	3	26
Housewives (i.e. not otherwise employed) (123)	0	123	123
Lawyers: (43)			
Judges	19	0	19
Practicing Attorneys	18	6	24
Military Officers (22)	22	0	22
Physicians (29)	18	11	29
University Professors and Administrators (29)	16	13	29
Writers, Journalists, Editors (28)	13	15	28
	235	202	437

Our businessmen were of two kinds, "organization men" and entrepreneurs. The organization men, working for the large corporations, were all in the senior executive category with salaries (which may not represent total income) of $25,000 and up—mostly up. The independent, small businessmen were sole owners, partners, or top managers. Military personnel had all achieved the rank of Lieutenant Colonel or higher in the Army or equivalent ranks for the other services. Medical practitioners were all specialists with prominent hospital connections, research connections, or other evidences of leadership in the profession. The attorneys were either partners in well-known law firms or were in the employ of large corporations or top governmental agencies. The judges all presided over appellate courts. Nonjudicial state government officials were all at least of cabinet rank or were first assistants to men of cabinet rank. Federal appointive persons were all in a salary category over $20,000 and held positions which had obvious policy-forming aspects. Clergymen were either in high ecclesiastical positions or, if local pastors, held pastorates in churches which had more than local reputations. Professors all held full professorial rank, had national eminence as writers, consultants, or as scientists, or held key administrative positions in high-ranking universities.

All of the men were college graduates and on the average had completed one and one half years of formal education beyond the A.B. degree. As might be expected, graduates of well-known eastern universities predominated, as did also those from the more prestigious schools in the rest of the country.

The eligibility of women was determined in either of two

ways. Single women were judged by the same criteria as were used for men. Married women were presumed to hold the social-economic ranking of their husbands; widows and recently divorced women, the ranking of their former husbands. Women were more heterogeneous than men with respect to education—a few had not completed college while others were as highly educated as any of the men.

The marital status of the persons selected for interview compares closely to that of the total American population in the middle years.

Present Marital Status of Persons Interviewed

Married:		406
First marriages	313	
Second marriages	76	
Third marriages	17	
Unmarried:		31
Divorced	15	
Widowed	4	
Never married	12	
	437	437

The people were all residents of metropolitan areas, although many lived in suburbs and some in remote exurban locations. They were all, however, occupationally and socially a part of some large metropolitan center.

People of all the principal religious faiths, as well as the unaffiliated and the nominally affiliated, were included, roughly in proportion to their representation in the total American population.

All the interviewees were between the ages of .thirty-five and fifty-five. This choice was made because we were interested in the experiences and reflections of mature people, who were still in the prime of their successful years.

We have interviewed in all, then, 437 men and women in the categories described. Our original intention was to interview five hundred, but shortly after we reached four hundred we noted that we were securing no new information. We were just piling up more and more instances of what we had already been told. We nevertheless continued for another thirty-seven interviews, then stopped, since it appeared that within the limits of our procedure we had apparently found out all we could.

Religious Classification of Interviewees

Protestant	213
Catholic	130
Jewish	27
"Nominal" (i.e. now totally inactive but formerly active in some religious organization)	46
No organized religious connection ever	21
	437

The Interviews

We obtained the information for the collective self-portrait of these people by adapting a type of inquiry not much in current use by contemporary social scientists—the unstructured, lengthy, and intimate interview. We used no schedule of formal questions—we simply engaged each person in informal conversation on the general subject of men and women and their relationships. Each person was interviewed separately, sometimes by both authors together, occasionally by only one.

The interviewees were allowed the widest latitude as to what they chose to discuss. The amounts of information we received therefore varied enormously. The shortest interview (few were this short) lasted around three hours. The longest took several days—a total of almost a week of intermittent interviewing. It would be possible in a number of instances to write a whole book with the information we have about a given person or a given pair.

We had anticipated that many of the people we intended to approach would be unwilling to discuss the subject of men and women with candor and originality. We could not have been more wrong. There were only two refusals; the rest talked freely and at great length. We had not been interviewing long before we discovered that our interviewees, once they trusted our purpose, were able and willing to give us information beyond what we had dared hope for. Over and over again they said they wished to cooperate with an attempt to get at the truth and were willing, even eager, to give private facts in confidence so that an accurate presentation could be made. While they recognized the need for pretense and concealment in their private lives, they also wanted to take part in a sincere and honest attempt "to look behind the masks."

After several hours of interviewing, a corporation executive said:

> My first impulse, I guess, was to answer a few questions for you and be on my way. But I got carried away with this thing. You seem to be up to something more honest and complete than the stuff I've read on this subject. There's a lot of humbuggery that

passes around for truth.... I even tried to do that with you at first. But I got carried away with the idea that some good could come of this. And even if it doesn't, it's quite an experience to sit down and talk for all these hours. When you've talked to as many people as you say you're going to, you should have a goldmine of information and I'm glad to contribute my bit to clearing up some things that are long overdue....

I don't know why I've trusted you with all of this —my God—you could blackmail me—but I know you won't, any more than my doctor or my priest would. ... If you want to repay me, just write a damned honest book....

In these conversations we used very little direct interrogation, except for such publicly verifiable items as occupation, age, place of residence, religious affiliation, amount and kind of college education. To get the interviewee started, we employed a few standard catalytic questions—questions which asked for nothing in particular, but were designed to find out how the subject was oriented to larger questions. One which proved particularly effective when speaking with women was, "Well, what's it like to be a woman these days?" Such a question asks everything and nothing at the same time. To a woman with a bad marriage it might orient her to her entrapment; to an educated woman with career desires and a brood of preschoolers, it might mean something else; to a woman with a philandering husband, something else again; and so on. An opening question with men which proved effective was, "What do you think about marriage?" Sometimes we took advantage of a conversation piece from the current news in order to break in.

Once the subject started talking, we used chiefly what non-directive clinicians call "projecting feeling" as a way of participating in the interview without influencing its direction. For example, if the man was complaining about the dullness of his wife and then paused, one of the interviewers would say, "Oh yes, I guess some men do find their wives pretty dull." Almost invariably this had the effect either of causing the interviewee to turn to a new subject or to voluntarily compare himself to other people.

We also sometimes related fragments from other interviews in order to induce the current subject to be more explicit about his own views. In comparing himself to someone else he often gave more precise information in order to clarify his behavior and beliefs. At times the interviewers, seemingly spontaneously, started a mild disagreement between themselves concerning some point pertinent to the conversation. This usually would involve the interviewee further in the discussion and he would give additional illustrations from his own life. In one of our discussions of infidelity an attorney responded:

> No, the reason I'm agreeing with him (another interviewee whose wife had been unfaithful) is that a couple of years ago when I thought my wife was sleeping around with our pediatrician, I was inclined to raise hell at first, but the longer I thought about it— well, she wasn't doing anything I hadn't done, so maybe it would be just as well to try to be rational about it.

In sum, our efforts were devoted to keeping the interview more like an informal, intimate conversation among equals who had a serious interest in some matter. We were careful to avoid the role of expert (we were merely "inquirers") and, of course, took care not to offer any advice or interpretation or judgment about anything which the man or woman had discussed.

Interviewing in this mode yields material rich in detail, wide in scope, varied in color and intensity. This is in sharp contrast to the kind of information gained from questionnaires and statistical studies, or from interviews employing a uniform set of questions such as Kinsey used. While the Kinsey procedure secured precise and useful information which could be presented in neat tabular form, it told us little about the context in which the behavior occurred and nothing about the feeling dimension which is certainly at the heart of much male-female interaction. Moreover, Kinsey focused on the narrowly sexual. We focused on the total relationship, much of which goes far beyond the strictly sexual. (Kinsey himself was quite aware of these possible varieties in procedure and focus and acknowledged, as early as 1949, the need for a more holistic inquiry.)

Our procedure, then, while it is not magnitudinal, enables us to study relationships more fully. If we had asked 437 people, "Do you feel satisfied with your present spouse? Answer 'Yes' 'No' 'Uncertain,' " we would have had, of course, a tabulation of those who answered yes or no or were uncertain. But we would know next to nothing about how the subject felt about it, how much he had previously thought about it, what factual basis he thought he had for his judgment, or what, if anything, he intended to do about it. The most serious omission would be in our <u>not knowing the importance</u> <u>this particular fact, even if accurately reported, had in the</u> <u>person's life.</u> In contrast, we allowed the interviewee complete freedom concerning what he chose to discuss and what seemed important to him to say about it. We wanted to know from him only those matters about the world of men and women which were on *his* mind, about which *he* had important judgments or experiences, and not what *we* decided in advance might be important to ask.

This technique, of course, results in incomplete information in a statistical sense, since it underrepresents the number of people who experience a certain problem or hold a certain view or perform a certain act. For example, there is very probably a higher incidence of frigidity among these people than they reported to us, because if the problem was minor or if some satisfactory expedient had been worked out, there would seem to be little need to talk about it, and very likely other aspects of life would be discussed instead. Thus, we have not received *all* of the pertinent information which they might give us, but by this method we have secured the information which *they* considered important in their own life experiences.

The Hidden Dimension

We make no claim that this study, despite the intimacy of the material provided, gives the much-sought "whole story." Probably the whole story on most important matters is a mirage anyway. Particularly where human conduct is concerned, there is always a hidden dimension. Most informed people today realize that they are moved by forces which they do not understand or cannot even identify and that they use defenses to make their conduct appear acceptable to themselves as well as to others.

There was very general recognition among our 437 that there is a submerged part of their mental-emotional lives and that whether they try to understand it or not, they are profoundly influenced by it. "I don't really know why I . . ." "I suppose I'm rationalizing now, but . . ." "The id will out, you know . . ." are typical of remarks sprinkled liberally throughout the interviews.

There is no reason to doubt, then, that in their descriptions of their problems and predicaments, their perceptions and judgments have sometimes been colored by factors which they do not understand. Nor do we doubt that their adaptations, successful or otherwise, may sometimes have been rationalized to us, as to themselves, to make their life circumstances more palatable. Their testimony must be presumed to manifest human distortions in perceptions and judgment. But all these are part of the human condition and of the total reality which we are trying to comprehend.

The "Rashomon" Principle

One outcome of the hidden dimension is that people perceive reality differently. A man experiences what he perceives and what he feels, whether or not someone else perceives as he does and whether or not "pure objectivity" would call for another definition of the situation. If a man considers a woman beautiful, he *is* experiencing a beautiful woman, whether or not a panel of beauty contest judges would so rate her. If he feels insecure because she is so beautiful and he fears he may lose her to another man, this fear and insecurity is a part of his world, whether or not someone else judges that such a risk exists. The woman herself may feel securely and eternally mated to him and be contented and thrilled with his masculinity. But if he feels upstaged by other men, he may live, make choices, and anticipate the future only in terms of these realities of life as they exist for *him*.

There is no escaping the practical importance of the subjective nature of reality. When one makes decisions, renders judgments—in fact, whenever he thinks, or even when he acts unconsciously—his mental processes can deal only with the perceptions which *he* has had. When one is examining the intimate side of people's lives, their hopes, their fears, their conceptions of themselves and the significant others in their lives, he is unavoidably involved with this *Rashomon* principle.

Compassion consists in part of the ability to understand that this is necessarily so. If a man thinks his wife is an inveterate flirt, then as far as his mental-emotional life is concerned, she *is* an inveterate flirt. A private detective's report on her conduct, accompanied by legal proof, might, to someone else, constitute objective evidence to the contrary, but unless and until the man accepts such evidence as the truth, he is in fact *experiencing* a flirtatious wife. Thus, such words as oversexed and undersexed, masculine and feminine, exploitative, frigid, can have meaning only in the specific context of each person's own hidden dimension. One man may beat his wife and still convince her that he loves her. Another man may offer the mildest criticism to his wife, from which she concludes that, since he says such horrid things, he doesn't really love her.

There is a tendency to regard such perceptions as unfortu-

nate, as weakness of the intellect or inefficiency in mental
operation. Distorted perceptions, however, also have a positive function. The man married to a plain Jane who thinks
her beautiful may be adding a dimension to his existence
which enriches his life as well as hers. A man who thinks
of himself as more masculine than collective judgment
might grant, may, because of this feeling, introduce a confidence into his interaction with women which could easily
bring out more charm and basic sexuality—to everyone's benefit. Thus, it is a moot question whether love is blind or
whether it is only those in love who really see. The line between distortion and objectivity is not only hard to draw, but
one often does not know which is which.

In our conversations with our 437 we were, of course, repeatedly made aware that there are alternative perceptions
and feelings about seemingly the same circumstances. We
have not, however, been primarily concerned with trying to
spot distortions and rationalizations. Rather, we chose to be
permissive and compassionate in the sense that we accepted
their feelings, beliefs, and judgments for the purpose of trying to determine how *they* view their world and what linkage
they see between their acts and their beliefs, their past and
their present. Each person's mental-emotional operations we
have accepted as having an intrinsic integrity, even if by conventional standards they might be considered strange or morally offensive.

Generalizations

During the five years of interviewing we painstakingly
avoided setting up classifications, formulating hypotheses, or
using any formal concepts in dealing with our material.

Thus, when the interviewing phase was completed, we were faced with the enormous problem of organizing and summarizing the raw data. Much of the verbatim testimony, because of the informal nature of the interviewing, included repetitions and extraneous subject matter. After sorting out such material, we turned our attention to capsuling the essential facts, sequences, circumstances, and viewpoints of each case. We spent nearly two years analyzing the several million words of testimony in order to discover the general outlines as they had been presented by these people. There were 437 variously complete portraits, no two of which were exactly alike, yet within the diversified detail we could see a number of patterns—recurrent situations, repeated dilemmas, parallel solutions—taking shape. Then we could at last move toward the analyses, of which this book consists.

While the dimensions of this inquiry are not magnitudinal, in the presentation of our findings it is difficult to avoid the conventional words: many, most, some, few. We have tried, however, to use such relative quantities cautiously and with unusual care. They are defined as follows:

few—recurrent but reported by no more than 5 to 10 per cent of the interviewees
some—a greater frequency than few, but not exceeding 25 per cent
many—a substantial minority, more than 25 per cent, but less than a majority
most—more than a majority
typically—used interchangeably with *most*

These terms are sometimes used to refer to the entire 437 and at other times to refer to a specific category or subcategory, as indicated by the context. Furthermore, they are to be understood as representing our best judgment in the matter and not necessarily an actual count.

Wherever possible we have tried to let the people tell their own story; *quoted materials are always to be understood as being representative of other people not quoted.* Unusual or unique situations or personalities, however interesting, have not been included in the analysis. This book, then, presents the sharings and hindsights and thoughtful explorations of 437 successful American men and women. It has been substantially written by them.

Chapter 2

PREACHMENT, PRACTICE, AND PRETENSE

ONE does not really understand a person in any important phase of his being until three dimensions are revealed—what he says, what he does, and how he fits the two together. He may be consistent, inconsistent, or variously equivocal about his pronouncements and his actions. And if there are discrepancies, he may or may not recognize them or feel obliged to resolve them. Whatever the configuration, however, the measure of the whole man involves all three.

Preachment: The Monolithic Code

The blueprint for correct conduct and right thinking about men and women is well known. This monolithic code is based on precepts from Judaic and Christian tradition and has long been codified into law and buttressed by something vaguely referred to as public opinion. Few, therefore, have to be told that chastity, fidelity, parenthood and various forms of attendant responsibility and restraint, all channeled through heterosexuality, are the mainstays of proper male and female conduct. There is little equivocation about this. After such a summary of the requirements of the code, a public relations executive, forty, concluded:

> Who am I to question the word of God? Even if I didn't believe in God, who am I to set myself up as a better authority than the history of the race? Even with my ego, I'm not up to *that* . . . We may or may not be children of God, but we better know what's good for us—and obey.

The more formally religious tended to put it more tersely: "It's the command of God," or "It's natural law."

The monolithic code is said to be practical too. A woman, who characterized herself as "really quite irreligious," stated the case in pragmatic terms:

> You've got to have an *order* for things. Even if it isn't perfect, you have got to have some clear-cut and uniform system for handling things like the care of children, care of women in pregnancy and afterward, provision for the infirmities of old age, inheritance, regulation of sex urges, legitimacy—a whole host of practical things. It would be simple chaos if we didn't all have to follow the system.

Further validation for the code comes from those who have followed the code faithfully—or nearly so—and feel that it has stood them in good stead. The benefits have been appreciable and they are grateful. Others could have these same benefits, they think, if they would only observe the code.

My wife and I came close—well, maybe not quite "close"—to divorce a few years ago. But we stuck it out. Later we grew up, I guess. Anyway, we are now genuinely in love; the old bickering and even the cheating are gone. If we hadn't just refused to take the easy, thoughtless, narrowly selfish way out, where would we be now? Alone—or married to someone else and in the same fix. We'd be guilty—bitter probably . . . and then, there's the kids . . .

Or again:

I wasn't nearly as wild as most of the girls in my sorority. And I'm glad of it now. You just have to realize that if you resist temptations to violate stand-ards—even though others do—in the long run you'll be glad for it—and really a lot better off. At fifty, how can I possibly be better off because I "expressed myself" freer when I was twenty? It's just not logical.

Those who do not or cannot conform to the code are variously the object of pity or censure, but in any event it is hoped that they will be unobtrusive. Violators, moreover, are presumed to be a minority and they ought to be contrite about it. One easily draws the further inference, reinforced by informal communication, that the ways of the transgressor are hard and that only the fools or the sick or the degenerate transgress.

The code is accepted, even honored, by those who have not shared in the fulfillments which it is supposed to bring. Some were embittered and hostile because they had not done well despite their efforts to follow conventional expectations, and they deeply resented the apparent successes of those who had departed from the code. They resented, for example, the middle-aged man or woman who found a second life through divorce, or the single man or woman who carved out a meaningful marriage-like relationship—especially when it is clear that these other people feel they are well off this way. Thus, a forty-year-old housewife, married to a prominent medical researcher, stated the familiar case forcefully:

> It burns me up to think of a man the age of my father waltzing around with a thirty-fiveish woman, going off to Bermuda for a honeymoon and coming back and picking up his practice just where he left off a few months earlier. I'll take his word for it that he had a difficult time with his first wife. I've had a difficult time with my husband too. And I suppose he does with me. But one simply isn't supposed to act like he's in his twenties when he's in his sixties. I hope he lives to rue the day.

History has spawned a plethora of apologists, rationalizers, and thundering prophets, each offering absolute reassurance that this is not *a* but *the* monolithic order. All reinforce one another in the tacit acknowledgment that the code is neither an hypothesis nor even an ideal; it is a proscription. Despite the dramatic re-shapings of thought and action during the present century, few men of stature, with exceptions like Bertrand Russell and Judge Lindsay, have risen to move important amendments to it.

Practice: Virtue and Vice

Practice, as everyone knows, does not necessarily follow the precepts of the preachments. A systematic look at the actual behavior of people, as distinct from casual talk, reveals clear discrepancies between the expectations of the code and the behaviors of many. For a variety of reasons many people do not heed the honored proscriptions, and those who do are not always living testimonials to its adequacy. Even though some have, in fact, followed the proscriptions of the code, they say by middle age that they regret having done so. The reflections of the wife of a nationally known physician illustrates one prominent pattern which we heard recurrently:

> Many of the middle-aged women I know complain that the fates cheated them—not me. I cheated myself. ... If this seems to have a strange twist—well, you can call it the testimony of a *nice* girl. ...
>
> Maybe I'd better get down to details. My father always insisted that I *was* a nice girl—even when I was bratty. But I never really let him down on the big things. ... The big test came in my junior year in college. I was deeply in love with a promising law student (he's now on the bench—Court of Appeals). We went further and further as lovers do. But when it came down to brass tacks, I chickened out. I remembered my father's "nice girl." Now, I was no prude. You can't be a sorority girl at ———— and not be involved in endless bull sessions on sex. I knew that all the girls "did"—or nearly so. And, as I said, I was no prude. I'd petted to climax lots of times—with two or three other

boys and often with him. But to go to New York for a weekend—I couldn't see it. I said No and meant it.

He said he was proud of me and of my standards and that he loved me all the more. In three or four years we'd be married. . . . Well, from that day on he slowly lost interest. You could feel it—the love-making lost its bang. Then we dated less and less often and then there was another girl and you can guess the rest.

But I got over it. I transferred to Home Economics teaching—even though my talent and love was still for Constitutional Law and History. Again, the "nice girl" —what would a woman do in *that* field? So I became a Home Ec teacher—that's the lost battalion of the de-womanized teaching corps! You're stereotyped—and damn it, so far as I can tell, the caricature is pretty well deserved.

So, I stayed with the anesthetized set for five years before another love turned up. This man was thirty and I was about twenty-five by then. Sex again! Believe me, I *wanted* to. He was matter-of-fact about it, but by no means crude. When I wouldn't, he politely dropped me with the comment that he should have known that I wasn't a whole woman. I began to doubt if I was, but I was still a Girl Scout at heart. . . .

For the next thirteen years? A scattered series of dates, some more or less erotic. Finally, in desperation one night, I did—and I found that I was *all* woman— I loved it! If I'd known how a man and woman can really be—how different it is from orgasm in petting, I'd have started back there when I was in college, when I had the chance to have *all* the parts of a man and woman together in one pair—and love too. By now, the pickings (for *love,* that is) are pretty slim. . . .

Anyway, at forty-eight I'm married to a very successful physician. He's fifty, a widower but still in love with his Mary. He's devoted to his kids and he's not in very good health. He married me for good reasons —for him. But I'm not complaining; I didn't have to. He has in me an efficient homemaker, an ego extension for entertaining and other protocol—and that's about all. There's no sex to amount to anything— quantity *or* quality. . . . But I'll stay with it—what else is there?

But if you or anyone else ever gives me that "wait for marriage," "guard your reputation" poison, I'm apt to say some very unladylike things—things I've had twenty years to rehearse. Those girls of my college days who acted as if they didn't give a damn for reputation *or* marriage are now married, mostly to Ivy League men, and have children of their own in high school and college. Oh, they've had their share of divorces and scandals and what not, but I'd trade my life for the worst of theirs in one second flat. Yes, including my roommate, now Mrs. Senator ————, with her two abortions during college! She and her husband are devoted to each other, live fully, and have two sons. I'm that "nice girl"—now fully employed as a baby sitter for a prominent doctor, with no children of my own, and a miserable sex life. But I should take comfort; I never let my parents down or violated my Scout oath. Can you match that for the life story of a damn nice girl?

We can. With quite a few. Details vary, of course, but the same general pattern keeps turning up: regret at having shunned certain disapproved conduct. We also found women, of course, who now regret their abortions or their adolescent wildness or their extramarital affairs, but a roughly equal number say that they now regret having followed the straight and narrow to the extent that they did. Furthermore, we found many more who regret *not* having divorced than who do regret their divorces. We found a few who say that if they had it to do over again they would have been chaste in the premarital years, but more, as in the interview just quoted, who feel that their chastity prevented them from getting the kind of start in the male-female world which most of their peers had. Some said that they now feel such experience would have been a good introduction to reality.

Regret and hindsight aside, how do the transgressors fare in the long pull? Do the dire consequences predicted for them actually occur? The following account in its general outlines is a familiar sequence among the Significant Americans—both men and women. This account begins with a letter written in early 1943 and published in a study shortly thereafter:

We were college "steadies" for six months with no mention of marriage. We weren't prudish, though I did remain a virgin. Then he was drafted and soon he proposed. We weren't alone for an hour before he was pressing the marriage issue. . . . I liked him very much . . . we did seem to have much in common. I doubted that I was in love but I couldn't prove it. . . . I don't remember just how it happened but I suddenly realized that I was no longer virginal and the pressure to get married was now greater than ever. . . . We were married and he then went back to camp. . . .

Then I received a letter from him stating that he had found a room for me near the camp. So overnight I packed a few belongings and boarded a train. And there I lived for three months a semi-prisoner. One and a half days each week were deliriously happy; five and a half were dismally lonely, like a prisoner in a foreign land. Then he received orders to move and I went back to my home community.

At first I was lonely. I moved in my old circle of friends. One day someone suggested that I go on a "date"—a purely platonic date, of course, with a fraternity brother of my husband. There being no harm on that date, there was another and another and suddenly they weren't so platonic. Gradually I began to realize that I was falling in love with this man and he with me. And accordingly we broke off the relationship, abruptly. Soon thereafter I discovered that I was pregnant—by my husband, of course. When I wrote the news to my husband he was very disturbed. I could understand him because I felt the same way. We had never really been truly married and both of us knew it. . . .

Meanwhile, I was haunted by my recently discovered relationship with the second man. I cannot justify it ethically but I feel it emotionally. . . . He finds it difficult to call our relationship off, even though he knows that I am pregnant and I strongly wish to remain loyal to my marriage. . . . I haven't the slightest idea how it will all turn out but I must confess, being as rational as I can, that I can see many possible outcomes but none that is satisfactory.

To continue with the next twenty years. An abortion was performed, against her husband's wishes, and they were soon divorced. To what extent the abortion figured in the divorce is not clear. Thereafter followed a period which she characterized as "an awful lot of wildness and promiscuity" during which, however, she advanced very rapidly as a chemist's assistant in a war plant.

I was intermittently enthralled by my career success and emotionally devastated by my immorality. But shortly, I learned to live with both.

She soon became so valued an employee that the corporation sent her to graduate school where she completed a Ph.D. degree, and has since become a scientist of national reputation.

All through this, my amorality continued—the only change was that I felt less and less guilty about it all.

About six years ago she married a man approximately her age, who had been widowed and had one child. The marriage was described by both of them as a "perfect union in every respect." She has continued with her career which is entirely distinct from his, although he holds an important position too. At the time of this writing, she is pregnant and eagerly looking forward to having "another child."

An outcome such as this gives the moralists among the Significant Americans trouble. We shared this account with a number of our interviewees, using it as a conversation piece to elicit their moral judgments. Some shrugged their shoulders, said simply that there is nothing remotely strange about it, that they know many people with essentially the same background, varying only in details. At the other extreme, there were those who were disbelieving: the woman must have lied; she must be "sick" or at least desperately unhappy. Others took comfort from the fact that she has *finally* "made it,"—their only regret being that it took her so long to straighten out.

Obviously, many interpretations are tenable in the light of confused moral and pragmatic judgments now so prevalent in American society; the Significant Americans give voice to all of them. On one point, however, the data give no quarter: evidence is abundant that there is no clear correspondence, for these people, between their observance or their defiance of the monolithic code and the way in which by middle life they have found fulfillment or unfulfillment, contentment or malcontentment.

The main difficulty which seems so often to have been posed for them is not so much that the monolithic code fails to present an attractive image of the good life; the trouble lies in its universalism, the tacit supposition that it prescribes the way in which *all* relationships between men and women must be ordered for everyone, regardless of circumstance, and that there is something inherently wrong, inappropriate, or dangerous in acting otherwise. If, as some of them have insisted, the monolithic code is "bankrupt," they see it as bankrupt not because it is lacking in the idealism which it holds up, but rather because it is too categorical a view of men, women, and their relationships.

A "great unlearning" (to use Abraham Myerson's apt

phrase) has occurred for many of them. Many said that eventually they recognized, either because of unfolding circumstances in their own lives or through observation of others, that the simplitudes which they had been carefully taught cannot be relied upon. Like the doctor's wife who did all the "right" things and "it turned out to be a great big nothing— or worse," they feel let down by the promise that failed. "So you're chaste and what do you get—a reputation for being a cold fish, a string of 'almost' love affairs, and a naiveté that compromises your marriage from the start. I tell you, it's a hoax." Some of the 437 have acted on new precepts and defend them because these have worked for them. They are content (or better) with their lives as they have worked them out. Others are openly hostile toward the monolithic code and say quite candidly that it contains "nothing of real worth for living in the real world of today. It's fanciful—like a pretty piece from Hans Christian Andersen."

Another large and articulate group lives on the other side of the divide. These are the people for whom no disturbance has occurred because the promise of personal fulfillment for following the code did in fact come to pass for them. They are neither disillusioned nor bitter, because all—or nearly all —has gone as the code seems tacitly to promise.

Maybe we're not exactly normal for this community (an Upper-Middle-Class exurban settlement about thirty miles from an eastern metropolitan city) but my wife and I are really pretty square—and we like it this way. I doubt either of us could live any other way, but neither of us has tried. You see, we were brought up to yield to the time-honored requirements of responsible living. That means to us respect for the God-given rules—but they don't seem like *rules*. We'd still be monogamous, care for the kids, love, honor, and obey if all the churches and all the laws were canceled tomorrow. That may strike you as a little odd because I've already told you that we don't belong to any church and I wasn't even brought up in one. Somewhere I learned the imperative of civil obedience—maybe overlearned it, judging by the people around here, but it has stood us in good stead for over thirty years now—and we aren't fixing to thumb our noses at so bountiful a blessing.

I get disillusionment enough in my profession (United Nations—formerly State Department) to fill my quota . . . Mind you, I'm not condemning anyone —that's *their* business. But for me and mine, our private life together is right out of the eighteenth century —and we're quite content this way.

Others, who have ordered their lives as this man has, told us that they cannot understand, despite an effort to do so, why there is so much "to-do" about men and women, why so many of their friends and acquaintances get divorced or become involved in "other relationships which always lead to trouble." Some are religious and feel quite confident that traditional, religious doctrines and moral precepts, reinforced by public opinion, contain the best guides for living. These people enjoy an appealing integrity and seldom need to worry about their own conduct in the light of monolithic standards. In short, they cannot really have it otherwise; they do not need to. What the experimenters call "the real world" has not required them to depart from the monolithic code to any appreciable extent.

In sharp contrast are those who have in important ways *not* lived in accordance with the monolithic code and who also acknowledge that they are not doing well in the male-female enterprise. They often link the two; to them their moral breaches and their discontent are causatively connected. A fifty-three-year-old retired military officer, now on the board of directors of a large corporation, sees it this way:

Now, I'm no bluenose—no fatheaded virtue peddler. But I'll bet someone would say I was—come to think of it, some have. I've been ribbed plenty for expressing these ideas before. Anyway, when I look back over my life where women and home and marriage and all that are concerned, I get pretty sad—and I blame myself, mind you, no one else. When I was young—say while at ———— (college)—I chased around a lot and got used to women of all kinds. Some were magnificent ladies—or at least became so later. Some were hot pieces—that's all they came to, really. Some were everything in between—smart ones too—real brains. I liked them all—and came to need them all. This went on until I first got married (at twenty-seven). That was a shock. I couldn't get used to one woman—no matter how good she was to me, I just couldn't be anything but on the look for something else. No woman pleases me in more than one way for long. . . . Well, she divorced me and I don't blame her a bit. I was a bastard and I know it. I should never have married again, but I did. The same damn thing

again. This lasted longer because I was stationed over-
seas and while there was free to do as I pleased—and
did. But when I retired—and even before, when I was
stateside—it just couldn't work. . . . Like a fool, I did it
a third time. . . .

Now here's how I have it figured. It all goes back
to those early years—nineteen to twenty-nine—when
I should have had hell kicked out of me for living off
the country the way I did. If somebody—my parents
or some friend or anyone—could have shown me what
kind of habits I was getting into, how impossible I was
making myself for a decent monogamous marriage,
I *might* have listened. But nobody did.

Now I'm caught both ways. A fifty-year-old man
ought to be married and have a home. And I want to.
But I can't break a lifelong habit to tramp around. No
woman will stand for it—not a decent one anyway—
and I can't be any other way. . . . A little discipline and
moral guidance would have made me a lot happier
man today.

These four cases roughly describe the parameters of the
private world for the 437. There is the woman, regretful of
her early conceptions of virtue, bravely if a little bitterly
facing up now to her lost opportunity and trying to live up
to the realities of position and public expectation. The second
woman with the prime years of her life spent flaunting almost
all parts of the code which applied to her, in later middle life
settling in to enjoy her career success and her late marriage.
Then the man living, and having lived, comfortably and
quietly, almost idyllically, in the comforting arms of tradi-

tion. Lastly, there is the man whose life has not "worked out," who thinks he was compromised by his willful disobedience of the code.

Life histories bounded by these parameters are, of course, not always so neat. Whether there is contentment or disillusionment, it is as a rule not clear-cut. There is usually at least some ambivalence either way. Yet, categorical niceties aside, the four theoretical combinations are all illustrated profusely in our data. *None of the four is a rare outcome; each is found repeatedly among the 437 protocols; none is predominant enough to warrant a confident conclusion* as to how people come by success or failure in the sphere of men and women.

Pretense: The Great Myth

To bridge the wide gap between their preachment and their practice many of the prominent persons whom we interviewed console themselves and each other by using a very practical and ancient device—pretense. While admittedly living *de facto* lives which are often in sharp contradiction to the monolithic code, they pretend nevertheless that the code is an adequate one by which to order the relations of men and women. Partly consciously and partly unconsciously they have evolved a rather elaborate mythology which enables most of them to live comfortably with the discrepancies between their affirmed belief in the code and their contrary courses of action.

By no means all share equally in the pretense. To some, like this woman editor, mother of an honor student now in law school, the code is

... merely a set of rules which one talks up on formal occasions and with people who don't really matter anyway. You sort of wallow around in a sentimental mishmash like Fourth of July speeches, some sermons, and college commencement speeches. Rare is the truly honest moment, but no harm is done. No one takes any of it seriously, anyway.

Some are openly cynical about it all. An accountant, turned business executive, describes the feeling:

It's what you *seem to be* and not what you really are and believe that is the key to acceptance by people. I'm always for God, morality, motherhood, and the sanctity of the American home. It's the most safe and the most profitable when I'm talking to anybody outside of my very private world. So, of course, I support the church and all its pretense, and the Boy Scouts, and I suppose if someone important came around to solicit, I'd make a contribution even to the W.C.T.U. —say, would you like a drink?

Still others are not really cynical toward the monolithic code; they merely see it as a prudent public relations front, which people in this class take for granted. In these terms some of those we spoke to told us they recognized that they lived in a Janus-like society, that one says one thing and acts another; others do too and no one should feel any need to be consistent. They see it, thus, as merely a kind of etiquette or discretion, as did this woman who was discussing her problems involving a teenage daughter.

So I keep it to myself—you know how people are—gossip and all. What they don't know won't hurt them. Whose business is it anyway but mine? Why should I leave the shades up? What I do privately is for me and mine. I let the neighbors do and think what they want to. That gives them and me the same protection, doesn't it?

Thus, she, like others, not only practices concealment but she also accepts the legitimacy of others' concealment from her in exchange for mutual privacy.

This barter in contrived innocence is reassuring, but some have lurking doubts:

I do at times wonder . . . what *does* go on in other people's lives? We all respect each other's privacy to the point where we're really ignorant. It's not that I want to pry into my friends' and relatives' and neighbors' lives—but it's that when I remain ignorant, I have no way of knowing what really is. . . . It gets close to home. Take Kirk (her son, twenty-six, an architect). He's not married. Every now and then he brings a girl around—never even mentions marriage. He's obviously contented with life. He takes a lot of trips for extended periods. Frank (her husband) thinks he takes a woman along. He has never even hinted it to me. It's not that I'm accusing him of anything—after all, he's old enough to know what he's doing and so are the girls. Maybe the way we brought him up—discreet and silent, you know—maybe that's what makes it necessary for him to keep us ignorant. . . . You know, I've never leveled with him—really. But you just can't let your son know that you married his father because you were pregnant and that you've had a couple of affairs. . . . It's just not done, is it?

There are also those who try to "cut through the nonsense and see things as they really are," as a public relations consultant with a Ph.D. in psychology said:

> You know that's hard to do. Of course I'm scared, with two attractive daughters in college, but I'd be a plain damn fool not to realize that virgins by college age are almost extinct. And those few who remain are probably psychologically sick. My girls may get into trouble and if they do, I'll do my best to bail them out, but there's no point to pretending they're so innocent. . . . At the office too, I don't see how *anyone* can miss the sleeping-around of all kinds that goes on.

In sharp contrast, some present stark, almost schizoid, caricatures. One such man is a prominent sales executive for a large corporation. He is very actively religious and vigorously supported the monolithic preachments early in the interview.

> Marriage is a sacred thing. Our mystical union is a thing of God. On our knees each night we take our deep personal concerns to Him. Then we can go to sleep relaxed, unafraid. . . .
> Love between a man and a woman is the love of God—it's mysterious, beautiful and the wellspring of life.

Later in the interview he described an elaborate plan he had devised for the seduction of a colleague's "well-stacked" secretary, concluding with a detailed description of a torrid motel scene which would do honor to a pulp-writer. His repertoire of anecdotes and jokes on clear and consistent anticode themes was impressive both in color and in volume. This man is not at all unique among the Significant Americans. His type is matched very closely, for example, by a woman, also prominent and respected in church, civic, and welfare circles, who explained to us with much relish how one of her friends, ". . . a board member of ———— too, got herself screwed upstairs in the stable one afternoon by her trainer. . . . Gee, he *is* handsome though."

We heard the word, "hypocrite" every now and then applied to people such as these. In some cases "hypocrisy" does seem to be the correct word. But not always. Hypocrisy implies awareness and a deliberate intent to deceive. Pretense may be compounded of more honest psychological stuff. The true believer sincerely thinks that his views and the practical courses of action which follow are right; meanwhile in another compartment of his mind, he recognizes alternatives and may actually live by them. Yet he feels no need to alter his original mind-set. Each compartment is "logic-tight"—cut off from the other so that he feels no obligation to reconcile the two.

There are some, of course, for whom little pretense is necessary—those who are genuinely and deeply austere about the conduct of men and women. Sex and its various ramifications is to them an almost grim business. The implication in at least some formulations of the code that sex for adult men and women ought to be mostly a means to reproduction seems to some to constitute a clinching argument. A well-educated mother of several children, who described herself as being "not particularly religious," said:

> You have to remember that the Creator made men and women for something else than their own convenience and pleasure. But, good or bad, a marriage is only a means to an end. I know this sounds corny in a way but my husband and I both deeply believe that too much pleasure seeking and not enough deep responsibility to what male and female really exist for, is at the heart of a good deal of trouble with both men and women. . . . They all know it too—in spite of what they say and do. They're just like children who disobey and selfishly pursue what they want at the time.

Not everyone sees it so clearly however, and despite the crude concealments, discreet privacy, and the elaborate etiquette and euphemism, almost everyone among those we interviewed acknowledges that there is a "lamentable amount" of transgression of the monolithic code. But there is at the same time among many of them a stubborn reluctance to accept its frequency as reported by careful researchers, such as Kinsey. Disbelief, or at least the assertion of such, seems to be a part of the pretense. Said a modish, confident woman:

> One of the networks tried to pass off as true the ridiculous falsehood that several million American women—married ones, mind you—get abortions every year. I just won't listen to such programs—and I won't discuss the matter.

But she was quite willing to speculate on the alleged lurid consequences of divorce, adultery, or almost anything else. (This from a woman who holds a graduate degree from a distinguished university and enjoys a successful career as a scientist.)

And some have their whipping boys. A business executive, fifty-three, with a graduate degree in business from Harvard, wasn't very complacent either about transgressors or about those who, he felt, traffic in it:

> It's guys like you raising questions like this—and Kinsey too—that are responsible for all this to-do about marriage. Yes, and the movies; in fact, literary people in general—playwrights, novelists, poets—and all belly-aching about the world as it is and glorifying all kinds of forbidden fruits. It's getting so that a guy has to be ashamed of showing restraint and taking his marriage vows seriously. . . . If married people were just left alone, without these constant hints that things might be better "if" . . . Doubts and temptations are manu-factured. . . .
>
> I don't see any reason for granting anybody a divorce under any circumstances. The whole lot of psychiatrists and marriage counselors and psycholo-gists just stir people up anyway. It's right in the Bible somewhere—"When I became a man, I put away child-ish things" or something like that. Now why the hell can't men be men and women be women. If they get married, they stay that way. If a woman loses her shape with a few kids and a man grows a pot, why be surprised? They've been doing it for centuries. So you

have a fight now and then. Work it out instead of running away, I say.... Yes, my wife feels this way about it too. Life is no picnic anyplace and there are a lot of things we've got to be thankful for—the kids, our health, a good job, a nice community, and a secure future. What more is there?... No, I don't think I'm typical....

One man of forty, a driving and successful editor, added his voice to the argument against divorce while building an elaborate and deep pretense into his own life:

We married on the basis of a few days' courtship and probably didn't make the best choice. I'm forty and I still feel a strong urge when I see a young and attractive woman—and I've acted on it now and then—but (through clenched teeth and with a doubled fist) my wife and I agree on one thing—we've told each other that we would *never* get a divorce, on account of the children. They must never know—*never*.

These various forms of pretense seem to add up, then, to a colossal unreality—if not quite a myth—about how men and women in fact live and what they privately think about their own and others' conduct. This collective pretense, as we have seen, forms a reasonably tight logical system: the traditional ideas are said to have the supreme sanction of history and the Deity. They provide a practical arrangement for handling the consequences of heterosexuality. The number of people who are not held to the traditional code is systematically underestimated, partly because of concealment and partly by the general refusal to accept even those realistic exposures which are true. Meanwhile, erroneous assumptions are current regarding the necessary consequences of nonadherence to the code. All is reinforced by secrecy—sometimes even among supposed intimates. Some find the code completely adequate—at least in the ways in which they implement it. So the code is "believed" and asserted to be true, sometimes by the same people who have made a shambles of it in their own lives. It remains nominally enforced, in theory, by legal and ecclesiastical institutions. And it is hopefully, if not always confidently, taught to children.

Practically all of the remainder of this book documents the details of the contradiction between the monolithic code and the actual behaviors of actual people. A few juxtapositions have already been presented in this chapter: observance of the code does not in fact assure that one, or two, will find a good life thereby. And in many cases violators of the code do not necessarily get into any appreciable difficulty, psychologically *or* practically.

If all this seems confused and enigmatic, the Significant Americans nevertheless have it under control. As we shall subsequently see, they have their own paths cut through the tangled underbrush of opinion and counter-opinion.

Chapter 3

FIVE KINDS OF RELATIONSHIP

THE qualitative aspects of enduring marital relationships vary enormously. The variations described to us were by no means random or clearly individualized, however. Five distinct life styles showed up repeatedly and the pairs within each of them were remarkably similar in the ways in which they lived together, found sexual expression, reared children, and made their way in the outside world.

The following classification is based on the interview materials of those people whose marriages had already lasted ten years or more and who said that they had never seriously considered divorce or separation. While 360 of the men and women had been married ten or more years to the same spouse, exclusion of those who reported that they had considered divorce reduced the number to 211. The discussion in this chapter is, then, based on 211 interviews: 107 men and 104 women.

The descriptions which our interviewees gave us took into account how they had behaved and also how they felt about their actions past and present. Examination of the important features of their lives revealed five recurring configurations of male-female life, each with a central theme—some prominent distinguishing psychological feature which gave each type its singularity. It is these preeminent characteristics which suggested the names for the relationships: the *Conflict-Habituated*, the *Devitalized*, the *Passive-Congenial*, the *Vital*, and the *Total*.

The Conflict-Habituated

We begin with the conflict-habituated not because it is the most prevalent, but because the overt behavior patterns in it are so readily observed and because it presents some arresting contradictions. In this association there is much tension and conflict—although it is largely controlled. At worst, there is some private quarreling, nagging, and "throwing up the past" of which members of the immediate family, and more rarely close friends and relatives, have some awareness. At best, the couple is discreet and polite, genteel about it in the company of others—but after a few drinks at the cocktail party the verbal barbs begin to fly. The intermittent conflict is rarely concealed from the children, though we were often assured otherwise. "Oh, they're at it again—but they always are" says the high school son. There is private acknowledgment by both husband and wife as a rule that incompatibility is pervasive, that conflict is ever-potential, and that an atmosphere of tension permeates the togetherness.

An illustrative case concerns a physician of fifty, married for twenty-five years to the same woman, with two college-graduate children promisingly established in their own professions.

You know, it's funny; we have fought from the time we were in high school together. As I look back at it, I can't remember specific quarrels; it's more like a running guerrilla fight with intermediate periods, sometimes quite long, of pretty good fun and some damn good sex. In fact, if it hadn't been for the sex, we wouldn't have been married so quickly. Well, anyway, this has been going on ever since. . . . It's hard to know what it is we fight about most of the time. You name it and we'll fight about it. It's sometimes something I've said that she remembers differently, sometimes a decision—like what kind of car to buy or what to give the kids for Christmas. With regard to politics, and religion, and morals—oh, boy! You know, outside of the welfare of the kids—and that's just abstract— we don't really agree about anything. . . . At different times we take opposite sides—not deliberately; it just comes out that way.

Now these fights get pretty damned colorful. You called them arguments a little while ago—I have to correct you—they're brawls. There's never a bit of physical violence—at least not directed to each other—but the verbal gunfire gets pretty thick. Why, we've said things to each other that neither of us would think of saying in the hearing of anybody else. . . .

Of course we don't settle any of the issues. It's sort of a matter of principle *not* to. Because somebody would have to give in then and lose face for the next encounter. . . .

When I tell you this in this way, I feel a little foolish about it. I wouldn't tolerate such a condition in any other relationship in my life—and yet here I do and always have. . . .

No—we never have considered divorce or separation or anything so clear-cut. I realize that other people do, and I can't say that it has never occurred to either of us, but we've never considered it seriously.

A number of times there has been a crisis, like the time I was in the automobile accident, and the time she almost died in childbirth, and then I guess we really showed that we do care about each other. But as soon as the crisis is over, it's business as usual.

There is a subtle valence in these conflict-habituated relationships. It is easily missed in casual observation. So central is the necessity for channeling conflict and bridling hostility that these considerations come to preoccupy much of the interaction. Some psychiatrists have gone so far as to suggest that it is precisely the deep need to do psychological battle with one another which constitutes the cohesive factor insuring continuity of the marriage. Possibly so. But even from a surface point of view, the overt and manifest fact of habituated attention to handling tension, keeping it chained, and concealing it, is clearly seen as a dominant life force. And it can, and does for some, last for a whole lifetime.

The Devitalized

The key to the devitalized mode is the clear discrepancy between middle-aged reality and the earlier years. These people usually characterized themselves as having been "deeply in love" during the early years, as having spent a great deal of time together, having enjoyed sex, and most importantly of all, having had a close identification with one another. The present picture, with some variation from case to case, is in clear contrast—little time is spent together, sexual relationships are far less satisfying qualitatively or quantitatively, and interests and activities are not shared, at least not in the deeper and meaningful way they once were. Most of their time together now is "duty time"—entertaining together, planning and sharing activities with children, and participating in various kinds of required community responsibilities. They do as a rule retain, in addition to a genuine and mutual interest in the welfare of their children, a shared attention to their joint property and the husband's career. But even in the latter case the interest is contrasting. Despite a common dependency on his success and the benefits which flow therefrom, there is typically very little sharing of the intrinsic aspects of career—simply an acknowledgment of their mutual dependency on the fruits.

Two rather distinct subtypes of the devitalized take shape by the middle years. The following reflections of two housewives in their late forties illustrate both the common and the distinguishing features:

Judging by the way it was when we were first married—say the first five years or so—things are pretty matter-of-fact now—even dull. They're dull between us, I mean. The children are a lot of fun, keep us pretty busy, and there are lots of outside things—you know, like Little League and the P.T.A. and the Swim Club, and even the company parties aren't always so bad. But I mean where Bob and I are concerned—if you followed us around, you'd wonder why we ever got *married*. We take each other for granted. We laugh at the same things sometimes, but we don't really laugh together—the way we used to. But, as he said to me the other night—with one or two under the belt, I think—"You know, you're still a little fun now and then.". . .

Now, I don't say this to complain, not in the least. There's a cycle to life. There are things you do in high school. And different things you do in college. Then you're a young adult. And then you're middle-aged. That's where we are now. . . . I'll admit that I do yearn for the old days when sex was a big thing and going out was fun and I hung on to every thing he said about his work and his ideas as if they were coming from a genius or something. But then you get the children and other responsibilities. I have the home and Bob has a tremendous burden of responsibility at the office. . . . He's completely responsible for setting up the new branch now. . . . You have to adjust to these things and we both try to gracefully. . . . Anniversaries though do sometimes remind you kind of hard. . . .

The other kind of hindsight from a woman in a devitalized relationship is much less accepting and quiescent:

I know I'm fighting it. I ought to accept that it has to be like this, but I don't like it, and I'd do almost anything to bring back the exciting way of living we had at first. Most of my friends think I'm some kind of a sentimental romantic or something—they tell me to act my age—but I do know some people—not very darn many—who are our age and even older, who still have the same kind of excitement about them and each other that we had when we were all in college. I've seen some of them at parties and other places—the way they look at each other, the little touches as they go by. One couple has grandchildren and you'd think they were honeymooners. I don't think it's just sex either—I think they are just part of each other's lives —and then when I think of us and the numb way we sort of stagger through the weekly routine, I could scream. And I've even thought of doing some pretty desperate things to try to build some joy and excitement into my life. I've given up on Phil. He's too content with his balance sheets and the kids' report cards and the new house we're going to build next year. He keeps saying he has everything in life that any man could want. What do you *do?*

Regardless of the gracefulness of the acceptance, or the lack thereof, the common plight prevails: on the subjective, emotional dimension, the relationship has become a void. The original zest is gone. There is typically little overt tension or conflict, but the interplay between the pair has become apathetic, lifeless. No serious threat to the continuity of the marriage is generally acknowledged, however. It is intended, usually by both, that it continue indefinitely despite its numbness. Continuity and relative freedom from open conflict are fostered in part because of the comforts of the "habit cage." Continuity is further insured by the absence of any engaging alternative, "all things considered." It is also reinforced, sometimes rather decisively, by legal and ecclesiastical requirements and expectations. These people quickly explain that "there are other things in life" which are worthy of sustained human effort.

This kind of relationship is exceedingly common. Persons in this circumstance frequently make comparisons with other pairs they know, many of whom are similar to themselves. This fosters the comforting judgment that "marriage is like this—except for a few oddballs or pretenders who claim otherwise."

While these relationships lack visible vitality, the participants assure us that there is "something there." There are occasional periods of sharing at least something—if only memory. Even formalities can have meanings. Anniversaries can be celebrated, if a little grimly, for what they once commemorated. As one man said, "Tomorrow we are celebrating the anniversary of our anniversary." Even clearly substandard sexual expression is said by some to be better than nothing, or better than a clandestine substitute. A "good man" or a "good mother for the kids" may "with a little affection and occasional attention now and then, get you by." Many believe that the devitalized mode is the appropriate mode in which a man and woman should be content to live in the middle years and later.

The Passive-Congenial

The passive-congenial mode has a great deal in common with the devitalized, the essential difference being that the passivity which pervades the association has been there from the start. The devitalized have a more exciting set of memories; the passive-congenials give little evidence that they had ever hoped for anything much different from what they are currently experiencing.

There is therefore little suggestion of disillusionment or compulsion to make believe to anyone. Existing modes of association are comfortably adequate—no stronger words fit the facts as they related them to us. There is little conflict, although some admit that they tiptoe rather gingerly over and around a residue of subtle resentments and frustrations. In their better moods they remind themselves (and each other) that "there are many common interests" which they both enjoy. "We both like classical music." "We agree completely on religious and political matters." "We both love the country and our quaint exurban neighbors." "We are both lawyers."

The wife of a prominent attorney, who has been living in the passive-congenial mode for thirty years, put her description this way:

> We have both always tried to be calm and sensible about major life decisions, to think things out thoroughly and in perspective. Len and I knew each other since high school but didn't start to date until college. When he asked me to marry him, I took a long time to decide whether he was the right man for me and I went into his family background, because I wasn't just marrying him; I was choosing a father for my children. We decided together not to get married until he was established, so that we would not have to live in dingy little apartments like some of our friends who got married right out of college. This prudence has stood us in good stead too. Life has moved ahead for us with remarkable orderliness and we are deeply grateful for the foresight we had. . . .

When the children were little, we scheduled time together with them, although since they're grown, the demands of the office are getting pretty heavy. Len brings home a bulging briefcase almost every night and more often than not the light is still on in his study after I retire. But we've got a lot to show for his devoted effort. . . .

I don't like all this discussion about sex—even in the better magazines. I hope your study will help to put it in its proper perspective. I expected to perform sex in marriage, but both before and since, I'm willing to admit that it's a much overrated activity. Now and then, perhaps it's better. I am fortunate, I guess, because my husband has never been demanding about it, before marriage or since. It's just not that important to either of us. . . .

My time is very full these days, with the chairmanship of the Cancer Drive, and the Executive Board of the (state) P.T.A. I feel a little funny about that with my children already grown, but there are the grandchildren coming along. And besides so many of my friends are in the organizations, and it's so much like a home-coming.

People make their way into the passive-congenial mode by two quite different routes—by default and by intention. Perhaps in most instances they arrive at this way of living and feeling by drift. There is so little which they have cared about deeply in each other that a passive relationship is sufficient to express it all. In other instances the passive-congenial mode is a deliberately intended arrangement for two people whose interests and creative energies are directed elsewhere than toward the pairing—into careers, or in the case of women, into children or community activities. They say they know this and want it this way. These people simply do not wish to invest their total emotional involvement and creative effort in the male-female relationship.

The passive-congenial life style fits societal needs quite well also, and this is an important consideration. The man of practical affairs, in business, government service, or the professions—quite obviously needs "to have things peaceful at home" and to have a minimum of distraction as he pursues his important work. He may feel both love and gratitude toward the wife who fits this mode.

A strong case was made for the passive-congenial by a dedicated physician:

> I don't know why everyone seems to make so much about men and women and marriage. Of course, I'm married and if anything happened to my wife, I'd get married again. I think it's the proper way to live. It's convenient, orderly, and solves a lot of problems. But there are other things in life. I spent nearly ten years preparing for the practice of my profession. The biggest thing to me is the practice of that profession, to be of assistance to my patients and their families. I spend twelve hours a day at it. And I'll bet if you talked with my wife, you wouldn't get any of that "trapped housewife" stuff from her either. Now that the children are grown, she finds a lot of useful and necessary work to do in this community. She works as hard as I do.

The passive-congenial mode facilitates the achievement of other goals too. It enables people who desire a considerable amount of personal independence and freedom to realize it with a minimum of inconvenience from or to the spouse. And it certainly spares the participants in it from the need to give a great deal of personal attention to "adjusting to the spouse's needs." The passive-congenial ménage is thus a mood as well as a mode.

Our descriptions of the devitalized and the passive-congenials have been similar because these two modes are much alike in their overt characteristics. The participants' evaluations of their *present situations* are likewise largely the same —the accent on "other things," the emphasis on civic and professional responsibilities, the importance of property, children, and reputation. The essential difference lies in their diverse histories and often in their feelings of contentment with their current lives. The passive-congenials had from the start a life pattern and a set of expectations essentially consistent with what they are now experiencing. When the devitalized reflect, however, when they juxtapose history against present reality, they often see the barren gullies in their lives left by the erosions of earlier satisfactions. Some of the devitalized are resentful and disillusioned—their bitterness will appear at various points throughout this book; others, calling themselves "mature about it," have emerged with reasonable acceptance of their existing devitalized modes. Still others are clearly ambivalent, "I wish life would be more exciting, but I should have known it couldn't last. In a way, it's calm and quiet and reassuring this way, but there are times when I get

very ill at ease—sometimes downright mad. Does it *have*
to be like this?"

The passive-congenials do not find it necessary to speculate
in this fashion. Their anticipations were realistic and perhaps even causative of their current marital situation. In any
event, their passivity is not jarred when teased by memory.

The Vital

In extreme contrast to the three foregoing is the vital relationship. The vital pair can easily be overlooked as they
move through their worlds of work, recreation, and family
activities. They do the same things, publicly at least; and
when talking for public consumption say the same things
—they are proud of their homes, love their children, gripe
about their jobs, while being quite proud of their career
accomplishments. But when the close, intimate, confidential,
empathic look is taken, the essence of the vital relationship
becomes clear: the mates are intensely bound together psychologically in important life matters. Their sharing and
their togetherness is genuine. It provides the life essence for
both man and woman.

> The things we do together aren't fun intrinsically
> —the ecstasy comes from being *together in the doing*.
> Take her out of the picture and I wouldn't give a
> damn for the boat, the lake, or any of the fun that
> goes on out there.

The presence of the mate is indispensable to the feelings
of satisfaction which the activity provides. The activities
shared by the vital pairs may involve almost anything: hob-

bies, careers, community service. Anything—so long as it is closely shared.

It is hard to escape the word *vitality*—exciting mutuality of feelings and participation together in important life segments. The clue that the relationship is vital (rather than merely expressing the joint activity) derives from the feeling that it is important. An activity is flat and uninteresting if the spouse is not a part of it.

Other valued things are readily sacrificed in order to enhance life within the vital relationship.

> I cheerfully, and that's putting it mildly, passed up two good promotions because one of them would have required some traveling and the other would have taken evening and weekend time—and that's when Pat and I *live*. The hours with her (after twenty-two years of marriage) are what I live for. You should meet her. . . .

People in the vital relationship for the most part know that they are a minority and that their life styles are incomprehensible to most of their associates.

> Most of our friends think we moved out to the country for the kids; well—the kids *are* crazy about it, but the fact of the matter is, we moved out for ourselves—just to get away from all the annoyances and interferences of other people—our friends actually. We like this kind of life—where we can have almost all of our time together. . . . We've been married for over twenty years and the most enjoyable thing either of us does—well, outside of the intimate things—is

to sit and talk by the hour. That's why we built that imposing fireplace—and the hi-fi here in the corner. ... Now that Ed is getting older, that twenty-seven-mile drive morning and night from the office is a real burden, but he does it cheerfully so we can have our long uninterrupted hours together.... The children respect this too. They don't invade our privacy any more than they can help—the same as we vacate the living room when Ellen brings in a date, she tries not to intrude on us.... Being the specialized kind of lawyer he is, I can't share much in his work, but that doesn't bother either of us. The *big* part of our lives is completely mutual....

Her husband's testimony validated hers. And we talked to dozens of other couples like them, too. They find their central satisfaction in the life they live with and through each other. It consumes their interest and dominates their thoughts and actions. All else is subordinate and secondary.

This does not mean that people in vital relationships lose their separate identities, that they may not upon occasion be rivalrous or competitive with one another, or that conflict may not occur. They differ fundamentally from the conflict-habituated, however, in that when conflict does occur, it results from matters that are important to them, such as which college a daughter or son is to attend; it is devoid of the trivial "who said what first and when" and "I can't forget when you...." A further difference is that people to whom the relationship is vital tend to settle disagreements quickly and seek to avoid conflict, whereas the conflict-habituated look forward to conflict and appear to operate by a tacit rule that no conflict is ever to be truly terminated and that the spouse must never be considered right. The two kinds of conflict are thus radically different. To confuse them is to miss an important differentiation.

The Total

The total relationship is like the vital relationship with the important addition that it is more multifaceted. The points of vital meshing are more numerous—in some cases all of the important life foci are vitally shared. In one such marriage the husband is an internationally known scientist. For thirty years his wife has been his "friend, mistress, and partner." He still goes home at noon whenever possible, at considerable inconvenience, to have a quiet lunch and spend a conversational hour or so with his wife. They refer to these conversations as "our little seminars." They feel comfortable with each other and with their four grown children. The children (now in their late twenties) say that they enjoy visits with their parents as much as they do with friends of their own age.

There is practically no pretense between persons in the total relationship or between them and the world outside. There are few areas of tension, because the items of difference which have arisen over the years have been settled as they arose. There often *were* serious differences of opinion but they were handled, sometimes by compromise, sometimes by one or the other yielding; but these outcomes were of secondary importance because the primary consideration was not who was right or who was wrong, only how the problem could be resolved without tarnishing the relationship. When faced with differences, they can and do dispose of the difficulties without losing their feeling of unity or their sense of the vitality and centrality of their relationship. This is the mainspring.

The various parts of the total relationship are reinforcing, as we learned from this consulting engineer who is frequently sent abroad by his corporation.

> She keeps my files and scrapbooks up to date. . . . I invariably take her with me to conferences around the world. Her femininity, easy charm and wit are invaluable assets to me. I know it's conventional to say that a man's wife is responsible for his success and I also know that it's often not true. But in my case I gladly acknowledge that it's not only true, but she's indispensable to me. But she'd go along with me even if there was nothing for her to do because we just enjoy each other's company—deeply. You know, the best part of a vacation is not *what* we do, but that we do it together. We plan it and reminisce about it and weave it into our work and other play all the time.

The wife's account is substantially the same except that her testimony demonstrates more clearly the genuineness of her "help."

> It seems to me that Bert exaggerates my help. It's not so much that I only want to help him; it's more that I want to do those things anyway. We do them together, even though we may not be in each other's presence at the time. I don't really know what I do for him and what I do for me.

This kind of relationship is rare, in marriage or out, but it does exist and can endure. We occasionally found relationships so total that all aspects of life were mutually shared and enthusiastically participated in. It is as if neither spouse has, or has had, a truly private existence.

The customary purpose of a classification such as this one is to facilitate understanding of similarities and differences among the cases classified. In this instance enduring marriage is the common condition. The differentiating features are the dissimilar forces which make for the integration of the pair within each of the types. It is not necessarily the purpose of a classification to make possible a clear-cut sorting of all cases into one or another of the designated categories. All cannot be so precisely pigeonholed; there often are borderline cases. Furthermore, two observers with equal access to the facts may sometimes disagree on which side of the line an unclear case should be placed. If the classification is a useful one, however, placement should *as a rule* be clear and relatively easy. The ease is only relative because making an accurate classification of a given relationship requires the possession of amounts and kinds of information which one rarely has about persons other than himself. Superficial knowledge of public or professional behavior is not enough. And even in his own case, one may, for reasons of ego, find it difficult to be totally forthright.

A further caution. The typology concerns relationships, not personalities. A clearly vital person may be living in a passive-congenial or devitalized relationship and expressing his vitality in some other aspect of his life—career being an important preoccupation for many. Or, possibly either or both of the spouses may have a vital relationship—sometimes extending over many years—with someone of the opposite sex outside of the marriage.

Nor are the five types to be interpreted as *degrees* of marital happiness or adjustment. Persons in all five are currently adjusted and most say that they are content, if not happy. Rather, the five types represent *different kinds of adjustment* and *different conceptions of marriage*. This is an important concept which must be emphasized if one is to understand the personal meanings which these people attach to the conditions of their marital experience.

Neither are the five types necessarily stages in a cycle of initial bliss and later disillusionment. Many pairings started in the passive-congenial stage; in fact, quite often people intentionally enter into a marriage for the acknowledged purpose of living this kind of relationship. To many the simple amenities of the "habit cage" are not disillusionments or even disappointments, but rather are sensible life expectations which provide an altogether comfortable and rational way of having a "home base" for their lives. And many of the conflict-habituated told of courtship histories essentially like their marriages.

While each of these types tends to persist, there *may* be movement from one type to another as circumstances and life perspectives change. This movement may go in any direction from any point, and a given couple may change categories more than once. Such changes are relatively *in*frequent however, and the important point is that relationship types tend to persist over relatively long periods.

The fundamental nature of these contexts may be illustrated by examining the impact of some common conditions on persons in each type.

Infidelity, for example, occurs in most of the five types, the total relationship being the exception. But it occurs for quite different reasons. In the conflict-habituated it seems frequently to be only another outlet for hostility. The call girl and the woman picked up in a bar are more than just available women; they are symbols of resentment of the wife. This is not always so, but reported to us often enough to be worth noting. Infidelity among the passive-congenial, on the other hand, is typically in line with the stereotype of the middle-aged man who "strays out of sheer boredom with the uneventful, deadly prose" of his private life. And the devitalized man or woman frequently is trying for an hour or a year to recapture the lost mood. But the vital are sometimes adulterous too; some are simply emancipated—almost bohemian. To some of them sexual aggrandizement is an accepted fact of life. Frequently the infidelity is condoned by the partner and in some instances even provides an indirect (through empathy) kind of gratification. The act of infidelity in such cases is not construed as disloyalty or as a threat to continuity, but rather as a kind of basic human right which the loved one ought to be permitted to have—and which the other perhaps wants also for himself.

Divorce and separation are found in all five of the types, but the reasons, when viewed realistically and outside of the simplitudes of legalistic and ecclesiastical fiction, are highly individual and highly variable. For example, a couple may move from a vital relationship to divorce because for them the alternative of a devitalized relationship is unendurable. They can conceive of marriage only as a vital, meaning-

ful, fulfilling, and preoccupying interaction. The "disvital-
ity" of any other marriage form is abhorrent to them and
takes on "the hypocrisy of living a public lie." We have accounts of marriages which were unquestionably vital or total
for a period of years but which were dissolved. In some respects relationships of this type are more readily disrupted
because these people have become adjusted to such a rich
and deep sharing that evidences of breach, which a person
in another type of marriage might consider quite normal,
become unbearable.

> I know a lot of close friendships occur between
> men and women married to someone else, and that
> they're not always adulterous. But I know Betts—
> and anyway, I personally believe they eventually do
> become so, but I can't be sure about that. Anyway,
> when Betty found her self-expression was furthered
> by longer and longer meetings and conversations with
> Joe, and I detected little insincerities, not serious at
> first, you understand, creeping into the things we did
> together, it was like the little leak in the great dike.
> It didn't take very long. We weren't melodramatic
> about it, but it was soon clear to both of us that we
> were no longer the kind of pair we once were, so why
> pretend. The whole thing can go to hell fast—and after
> almost twenty years!

Husbands in other types of relationships would probably
not even have detected any disloyalty on the part of this wife.
And even if they had, they would tend to conclude that "you
don't break up a home just because she has a passing interest
in some glamorous writer."

The divorce which occurs in the passive-congenial marriage follows a different sequence. One of the couple, typically a person capable of more vitality in his or her married life than the existing relationship provides, comes into contact with a person with whom he gradually (or suddenly) unfolds a new dimension to adult living. What he had considered to be a rational and sensible and "adult" relationship can suddenly appear in contrast to be stultifying, shallow, and an altogether disheartening way to live out the remaining years. He is left with "no conceivable alternative but to move out." Typically, he does not do so impulsively or without a more or less stubborn attempt to stifle his "romanticism" and listen to well-documented advice to the effect that he should act maturely and "leave the romantic yearning to the kids for whom it is intended." Very often he is convinced and turns his back on his "new hope"—but not always.

Whether examining marriages for the satisfactions and fulfillments they have brought or for the frustrations and pain, the overriding influence of life style—or as we have here called it, relationship type—is of the essence. Such a viewpoint helps the observer, and probably the participant, to understand some of the apparent enigmas about men and women in marriage—why infidelities destroy some marriages and not others; why conflict plays so large a role for some couples and is so negligible for others; why some seemingly well-suited and harmoniously adjusted spouses seek divorce while others with provocations galore remain solidly together; why affections, sexual expression, recreation, almost everything observable about men and women is so radically different from pair to pair. All of these are not merely different objectively; they are perceived differently by the pairs, are differently reacted to, and differently attended to.

If nothing else, this chapter has demonstrated that realistic understanding of marital relationships requires use of concepts which are carefully based on perceptive factual knowledge. Unfortunately, the language by which relationships between men and women are conventionally expressed tends to lead toward serious and pervasive deceptions which in turn encourage erroneous inferences. Thus, we tend to assume that enduring marriage is somehow synonymous with happy marriage or at least with something comfortably called adjustment. The deception springs from lumping together such dissimilar modes of thought and action as the conflict-habituated, the passive-congenial, and the vital. To know that a marriage has endured, or for that matter has been dissolved, tells one close to nothing about the kinds of experiences, fulfillments, and frustrations which have made up the lives of the people involved. Even to know, for example, that infidelity has occurred, without knowledge of circumstances, feelings, and other essences, results in an illusion of knowledge which masks far more than it describes.

To understand a given marriage, let alone what is called "marriage in general," is realistically possible only in terms of particular sets of experiences, meanings, hopes, and intentions. This chapter has described in broad outline five manifest and recurring configurations among the Significant Americans.

Chapter 4

MISALLIANCE

A TRUISM, dating back at least to the Greeks, holds that satisfaction or fulfillment depends on one's expectations. Awareness of the connection between expectations and a sense of well-being is solidly documented in the testimony of our 437 people. Typically they admonish younger people entering marriage to hold to modest hopes. "They may think sex is fun now, but just let them wait a few years and they'll see. . . ." Another says simply, "An educated man doesn't get excited about anything. . . ." In one way or another they told us that the way to avoid disappointment is not to expect too much.

A minority, however, said that they overlearned this very lesson: they did hold their marital expectations low, but the dour philosophy did not sustain them and they now think that their error lay in not hoping for enough. This group of men and women talked forcefully about how they failed to respect sufficiently the urgency of their personal needs. They said that they did not then appreciate their untapped sexual potentials, or their capacity for mature love, or their acute need to be loved—"fully, creatively, and excitedly."

Two contrasting groups, then, are well represented among the 437—those who with the benefit of hindsight say that they hoped for too much and those who now say that they hoped for too little. It would be difficult to determine objectively which group has the greater sense of personal defeat by the middle years; the dimensions of frustration, like fulfillment, are hard to measure. Then, too, they have all made various unconscious adaptations along the way as they became aware of the discrepancies between expectations and realizations. There is the further complication that a person can at the same time hope for too much in one aspect of life and for too little in another; balancing out their total situations is not easy.

The interplay of expectation and realization is much more subtle, however, than simple speculative formulations would suggest. From the perspectives of middle life, many acknowledge that even when they did try to look ahead, they were not very clear about their own expectations before marriage or realistic about the nature of subsequent stages of marriage. In part, this resulted from the inadequacy of imagination and of education as guides to intelligent anticipation. Conventional descriptions of what is going to take place, and how and what one will feel, and what the problems will be, have been of little help, they told us. Manifestly some who did pray together did not in fact stay together; common interests between spouses for some became divisive and destructive of empathy; the coming of a child threatened and even destroyed some matings which previously were quite satisfactory; some men by getting more aggressive and romantic in their love-making drove indifferent wives further away.

Even when the conventional advice is statistically correct as stated, there is no assurance in the individual case, as we have earlier seen, that expectations based on them can be counted on. Statistically it *is* true that church-related people have lower divorce rates than the unidentified. This tells us nothing, however, about the *quality* of their marital relationships, and furthermore, a growing and not inconsequential number of church members do in fact become divorced.

Expectations are often interlaced with ambivalence. A State Department career man, now in his early fifties, had learned that ambivalence can set in early.

> In a very real sense I knew before I married her that I shouldn't. In some ways she was completely satisfying—like in bed. But in other ways I knew we were strangers and I knew it would get worse—but I had made a commitment—and besides she was virginal when I first met her—and then there was that damned betrothal announcement in the New York *Times* and the whole social superstructure that would have collapsed if we had broken up. All this was something at twenty-one I didn't have the guts to face. Now I'm facing a lot worse—but now I'm not a kid. But what can you do about it—*now*, that is?

Expectations can combine conventional but incompatible desires. As everyone knows, for example, there is sexual experimentation among the young and unmarried. It is not at all uncommon for men as well as women to admit to grave doubts that they can or want to give up sexual variety and become monogamous for the rest of their lives, even though they want to marry. A university administrator, who classed himself as happily married and a proud father, put the case bluntly.

This tying up of love, marriage, parenthood, and sex into one package is crazy for this century. They're all important, normal, healthy, and essential, really. But just because you love a woman and want her for a mother for your kids doesn't mean to me that you have to give up forever your right to sleep with another woman and enjoy her close companionship. If we hadn't agreed on that before we got married, we'd have stayed single. But the hell of it is that it's easier to agree on it and to act on it than it is to pull it off smoothly. Deep down you also feel that love *ought* to be enough—but then it isn't. It's a mess, isn't it?

Such sentiments are repeatedly documented in the unfolding of many of their lives.

There are also doubts about their capacity—especially among educated women—to find enough fulfillment in parenthood and domesticity to balance their isolation from a formerly satisfying career. A "domesticated journalist," as she called herself, was far from acquiescent.

Of course, you can beat yourself on the head and endure it, and you can hire help and you can hit the bottle. But can you really *like* it and find your *life* in it, the way I think my mother did? Well, I should have known I couldn't—and I haven't. And that's a pretty sad commentary on a woman's life.

Domesticity is often escaped through the employment of domestic help. But even so, the conventional expectations of others vex and accuse her, even though she doesn't fully agree with them. One woman with a successful gynecological practice feels the outside pressures.

My mother is practically ashamed of me. She thinks I'm an inferior mother. She has said that she wishes there was some way, without making too much fuss about it, that she could kidnap my kids and give them a decent upbringing. All she really means is that she wants to exercise her masochism on them. But I'm sure her ideas are in harmony with all her friends' and, I'm sure, some of mine. All of this just because I want to practice medicine and turn the children over to a very competent housekeeper who, by the way, knows more about running a house and bringing up kids than I do. . . . Sometimes, though, I do wonder if my mother isn't right about it. . . .

The subjects of the study explained to us not only that their expectations were fraught with conflicts within their own thinking and between themselves and others, but that they found a further complication—their expectations are constantly changing. Despite the acknowledged tendency for pairs to "grow together," to develop common habits and patterns and satisfactions, they often say that they underestimated the extent to which a pair remains two people. Thus expectations of some couples, which were reasonably consonant at the beginning of a marriage, may with the passing of time and the accumulating of experience become very different.

An attorney, working chiefly as a public relations consultant to a large corporation, was unusually clear about the alienation process.

> When we were first married, I think we agreed pretty well that there was a division of labor between men and women: that I was to support the family and she was to take care of it, that our home was to be a place of refuge from what I knew would be a rough world, and that she would take care of the children, be my mistress, and handle the protocol requirements of my position. In fact, we looked forward together to all this with a good deal of pleasant anticipation. But a lot happened along the way to our conceptions of what marriage and love are all about. She loathes protocol entertaining and I hardly blame her, but it's got to be done. She's bored to death with living in a world of psychological and mental inferiors. My career is even more taxing than I thought and our home is no refuge. I know she's cheating on me and I'm not sure I blame her, because I understand more than I have even admitted to her. You just can't figure it out, although I'm far more satisfied with things as they are than she is. . . . She has changed a great deal more. But then I suppose the worst strains were on her. . . .

While most of those interviewed acknowledged sexual experience prior to marriage, sexual awakening, especially for women, often came too late to influence mate choice; hence they gave it short shrift. Some, like this college honor student, discovered the error at thirty-eight.

I thought I knew what sex was. Gosh, I ought to have! ... But the truth of the matter is that I confused a kind of vague genitally located excitement, accompanied by intrigue, experimentation, and feeling that I was naughty, with the kind of earth-shaking experience I've later discovered. You just can't compare the two, and how are you supposed to know? I gather from talking with my friends that some women never get to this at all—and some of them find it outside of marriage—but an awful lot of us have made the discovery—and boy, is sex important now!

Sometimes the tardily awakened face up to the fact that they are going to have to pay a big price and take big risks in order to achieve the newly appreciated sexual satisfactions. In some instances, this means divorce or separation; in other instances, personal lives which, though the marriage is maintained, involve adulterous affiliations of various kinds. The possibilities and the outcomes are legion. Many face perpetual enigmas. Some are embittered. They vacillate between holding their husbands responsible, or themselves, or that vague but obtrusive outside reality they call "society." A mother of three school children voiced a repeated predicament:

I really don't know—should and can a sexually vigorous woman of forty renounce her sexuality for the rest of her life because her husband is away from home most of the time on business, and has a low sex capacity when he is here, and is uncreative and negative even about what little sex there is? *Who* says so?

Mismating

When the Significant American reflects on his choice of
marital partner, his conversation is often rich in colorful
details concerning the attributes of his mate, profuse with
comparisons and contrasts with others' spouses and with
other eligible persons from his past. An Ivy League law graduate related this candid, remorseful hindsight:

> If I'd thought enough about it before I got mar-
> ried, I'm sure I'd have made a better choice—but how
> is a kid of twenty-two supposed to know as much as a
> man of forty? I could have done a lot worse—that's
> for sure. But I could have also done a lot better. . . .
> You know, I think there are lots of second thoughts
> about choosing a woman. I've watched girls I knew in
> college grow up and get married and raise kids and
> *really mature*. And my rating of them *now* is a lot
> different from my rating of them then. Now, take
> Lee . . . she didn't send me much then, but today!
> There's a *whole* woman, I'll bet. . . .

His partner in the same law firm had a different hindsight:

> I either knew what I was doing back there or
> the gods were really with me. Anyway, there hasn't
> been a question in my mind from the day I proposed
> twenty-four years ago right up to today. That's one
> I called right—when you see what others are stuck
> with, you get grateful—very. (His wife said she wasn't.
> But she wanted to "be a good sport about it. I guess
> I could have done worse.")

Few people acknowledged that they had talked much together about each other's marital adequacy, but many more gave ample indication that they had thought about it alone or had discussed it in confidence with friends.

There is also the matter-of-fact acceptance of past decision —or at least a refusal to reflect on its adequacy or inadequacy. An executive editor phrased this position:

> What's the use hashing it over? It's done; so why rub it in? Better concentrate on things you can do something about. If you open up a subject like that, the first thing you know the whole matter will get magnified into a federal case and then you've *really* got a problem. Frankly, I don't know whether my wife thinks she married the right guy or not. I doubt she'd tell me any more than I'd tell her. If either of us gets too fed up, I'm sure we wouldn't be able to hide it for long, but it's not that clear-cut—at least not yet.

Psychiatrists and other analysts have often stressed that marital difficulties tend to be interpreted too largely in terms of the effects of a particular mate, and consequently that there is too much faith in solution by remarriage. *Divorce Won't Help,* says Dr. Edmund Bergler, for example, because the neurotic rigidities which plague the first relationship will persist and then harass the second.

Theologians, particularly Catholics, present the case in other terms. They point out that many marital frustrations spring from the imperatives of marriage and while somewhat differently experienced from person to person, are essentially the same, regardless of the specific spouse. One has

to endure serious inconveniences and anxieties associated
with child rearing, aging, illness, sexual difficulties, and myr-
iads of other matters, irrespective of who the spouse happens
to be. It is further claimed that improved character derives
from fortitude and from practicing some measure of ascet-
icism. So run the familiar arguments.

Regardless of debunking by psychiatrists or reasserting of
eternal verities by theologians, the Significant Americans typically believe none of them. They have a firm and unalter-
able belief that the right mating *is* of the essence—whether or
not they think they have one. They are sure that if all is
well in their pairdom, it is because they were lucky enough
or clever enough to have made a right choice.

> It's all quite simple. If you are happily married,
> you've got the right woman. If you aren't, you don't.
> What you do about it is another matter.

With the exception of the Catholics, and by no means all
of them, many boldly asserted that if serious marital frustration should occur for them, they would feel free to seek
another spouse. Also, they mostly said they would not "hold"
the present spouse, if he or she "wanted out." Their words
are sometimes braver than their feelings when called upon
to act, but these beliefs are exceedingly widespread and sincerely held. Many have in fact acted on them. A recently divorced woman, in the process of reestablishing her career as
a college teacher and "holding together" her preadolescent
children, explained:

> It's a matter of deep principle, you see. I felt no
> real need for the divorce. I was getting along all

right—nothing great, but all right. But if Bill wanted
out, he had the right to it. It hurt personally and it
was embarrassing socially. And it hurt when I considered the kids. But principle isn't supposed to be easy
to live up to.

When discussing misalliance as a source of difficulty, those
to whom we spoke typically rely on what they regard as a tell-
ing empirical test. They "know of cases," sometimes including themselves, in which some couple felt incompatible,
were divorced, each married again, and are allegedly happy
in the new marriage.

You see it all around—at work, in the neighborhood, at the country club, even at church. There's an
enormous part of every community that's made up of
happy, healthy, useful families in second and even
third marriages. Some of them went through hell for
a while, but they're in good shape now. (This man
is a Catholic business executive.)

Others said, however, that even though they accepted the
morality and the expediency of solving marital problems by
changing mates, they did not personally *act* upon such beliefs. The chief reasons given, as anyone might guess, were
refusals of the Church to sanction remarriage, "staying together for the sake of the children," and refusal of the spouse
(usually only temporary) to do his part in the necessary
collusion.

A minority, however, think they can demonstrate that
there is an exaggeration both of the seriousness of mismating

and of the benefits of remating. They say that many factors, apart from having a "wrong" spouse, are responsible for malcontentment in marriage and, morality quite aside, remarriage brings problems too.

> Look at my husband's partner. He thought his wife was too domineering, too attached to her mother, and didn't pay enough attention to him sexually. Most of us believed him—it certainly looked that way. So they got a divorce and look at him now. He remarried and he's all emotionally knotted up again. I think he feels more emotionally tied to his first wife—or maybe he's only guilty.... Now he's worried that he can't hold his new and beautiful wife. She doesn't dominate him but it looks to us as if he's a lost sheep—he just doesn't know how to manage his affairs himself. So now there are two sets of children and I suspect possibly some financial problems. They're far from content and there's his first wife lurking in the shadows. It's just no good.

Most of those who felt they were mismated wanted to talk about the reasons they chose the mate they did and how the unfolding of their lives brought them to their present awareness. Such efforts at self-examination and interpretation may be fraught with inaccuracies and self-deception, but they are still important since they constitute reality for these people and are the bases for present feelings and future courses of action. Summarizing their hindsights we found a few recurring explanations as to why they chose the wrong spouse.

. One theme was, "I should have been brighter."

I loused myself up at the start. She was a big sorority girl, prominent in student government, an honor student; but damn it, she's not very bright and she wasn't then. I think she was so manic that the professors, like me, thought she was bright. . . . For all practical purposes we have nothing in common. She's not such a poor housewife, as you can see. She has her strengths. She's still a party girl, even more glamorous than when she was in college (she is now forty-one)—it just takes her more hours to get ready now. She does decently well with the kids. She'd drive a perceptive mother wacky, but the kids do get fed and clothed and will probably grow up just as well. And she's a good housekeeper. And when you've said that, you've said it all. . . . Companionship, hell! For ten years we haven't talked about anything more important than the kids' grades or whether the budget will allow new draperies or whether we'll take a vacation this year and where. Damn it, let's face it, she's stupid and sometimes so embarrassingly so that I'd like to hide my face from my friends when she expresses herself on a serious subject. . . . So we lead a parallel sort of existence, like nursery school children in what they call parallel play. We're in the same room or in the same bed, but the physical fact is all there is. . . . No, we don't do much about it . . . too busy, too tired, not much opportunity anyway. . . . As for a more complete shake-up, I've no conviction that a new order would be worth the trouble of extricating us from this one.

... Sure, a lot of us are in the same boat; some guys
are better liars and some guys a little more lucky for
a while. ... And this thing you said someone called a
"vital" relationship—I don't know any, do you?) ——

If freedom of choice had anything important to do with
it, then the prominent persons we spoke to should have
chosen better mates. There was relatively little parental or
clerical dictation. Advice was freely given and cautions offered, to be sure, but each person was by strong custom free
to make his choice from a wide and loosely fenced field.
There was a free and easy association of the sexes from an
early age. Premarital sexual participation of varying amounts
and kinds was acknowledged. All this *should* have helped.

From what they told us, however, despite dating, courtship, and "going steady," they *now* feel that they were taken
in by their innocence (and also by their sophistication), by
their youth, and by the less-than-full honesty of each with
the other.

Where there were uncompromisable differences, typically
they had been there all along but were discovered too late.
The devastating part of this, they said, is that deep differences were covered over by various superficial similarities—
shared activities and feelings—which at first they found quite
congenial. Only after some time did the impasses become
clear to them. A physician said:

> A cutie who can toss the lines with you, get you
> stared at at the fraternity formal, whose daddy has con-
> vinced her that if she's coy enough there'll always be
> a man to take care of her, can be a hell of a lot of fun
> while you're living out your adolescence. But *grow up*

and her perpetual immaturity, her built-in inability to change from being a girly-girl, her childishness about the real world and the problems in it—why I've got another child, that's all. She needs more day-to-day wet-nursing than my twelve-year-old daughter. The girl I was so proud of and who did so many things with me in my twenties became an albatross around my aching neck.

A business executive:

It was all right when I was a flunky around the place. But when I moved up (senior executive) and had to take on social responsibilities and got to know some real women, she faded fast. I'm sorry, but it's that simple.

A clergyman:

We did try to be rational. Everyone told us—you must remember this too—to have fun while you're young, circulate, get to know quite a number of persons of the opposite sex; you may even raise a little hell now and then, but when you are ready to settle down, be sensible. We all got that advice from our parents and friends and even from the experts who write the books about love and marriage. . . . And when a marriage goes sour, people who make the post-mortems always seem to dredge up the cliché that if we had been more sensible, more rational, more practical when we chose our marriage partners, the grief and the wrench would not have been necessary. As for myself and a lot of my close friends, we can show you how you can get trapped just as easy by being sensible and careful as you can by being impulsive and emotional about love and sex and marriage.

Advice, some said, even when they heeded it, turned out to be more compromising than their recklessness.

Over and over women described one remarkably standard sequence. By the college years most of them had become sexually and emotionally aware and after some hesitancy experimented with sex one way or another. Then disappointments set in. There was simple fatigue or boredom; luck in partners took a turn for the worse, or sometimes there was exploitation, or only a suspicion of it. And choices, even for fun and escapade, were not always easy to condone on the morning after. A social worker, now an administrator in the federal Department of Health, Education, and Welfare, spoke for many as she explained:

> ... the quiet yearning for stable, meaningful things like home and children slowly tipped the balance too hard and too far and another kind of impulsiveness set in. The good, sensible, solid, stable, rational "catch" looked awfully good—and he turned out to be all of those things for sure. But later on you may like to return to the dance or to the romantic walk in the woods. But, oh no—you made another deal—you settled for a promising future and stability. He's so damned stable he hasn't read a poem or really listened to a song for twenty years. He sees life in terms of patients, pathology, and pocketbook. ... The good moral was overlearned by me—and a lot of other girls.

A theoretical physicist pushed his analysis a step further:

> If the considerations were reversed, if we all mar-
> ried for adventure and excitement, deep love and ful-
> fillment—if we made our mate choice in this way,
> there would be other risks, I'm sure, but we would at
> least thrill to the step and the touch of a mate instead
> of, as many of us now do, feel (at best) only security
> and (at worst) revulsion at the step and the touch.
> . . . You have to rely, I guess, on the fantasy at the art
> film or the cocktail party flirtation, or in the reality of
> some sort of escapade in which you get some facsimile
> adventure, excitement, thrill. The organization family
> for the red-blooded man or woman requires some kind
> of self-effacement that a lot of us just don't have.

Other men and women in the Upper Middle Class at-
tribute their current misalliance to the special imperatives
which they feel people in their position must heed. They
acknowledge, in short, that they used marriage as a means
to other ends.

> Your wife is important to your success—almost as
> much as you are. She's in the spotlight even more
> at times. She has important connections for you in
> this profession [lawyer working as an insurance corpo-
> ration executive]. Her pedigree, to put it bluntly, is
> enormously important. Her father can make or break
> you. That Horatio Alger stuff just ain't so. . . . And her
> best college friend may now be married to the junior
> partner in the firm. . . . You know all this when you

marry her and who can blame you if you try to help yourself by the right marriage? You open up doors in the same way as you do by going to the right college.

Women, too, told us that they had made similar miscalculations. They speak often of having been "sort of under pressure" from parents and peers to make an advantageous marriage.

My parents made a real sacrifice to send me to — (an exclusive Eastern college) during the depression. They were both educated, but they were not wealthy enough for that league. Somehow the idea got through to me that it was all worth the sacrifice if I could just marry "right"—not for frivolous personal excitement, but more for the glory of something or other. They were delighted when I brought home a proper Bostonian from Harvard—and would have been even if he had a hunchback and one eye. But a nice fellow of ordinary lineage and prospects—well, they'd grant he was O.K. But how about that other boy from Harvard? It gets to you after a while—and you accept it. You don't really look for the deep, personal things you should. You look for the valued externals and the personal things get short shrift. Why on my very wedding day I wasn't excited about our starting a vital personal life together—only about who was there and how the show looked. Even the honeymoon, apart from that grand trip, wasn't anything to get excited about. . . . Yet my husband was, and is, a fine man—able, moral, successful, and, as you know, quite famous now.

She went on to describe the details of an essentially lonely life.

> All of the externals I have, but the guts-level things I see in some other marriages aren't there. It's too much like we were faithfully living out the terms of a contract—although we *are* getting as much out of it as the covenant will allow.

These "alien motives" for marrying, as Max Lerner calls them in *The Unfinished Country*, take a variety of forms. Prominent are the marriages to "prove something"—by marrying the popular, rather than merely the "right" boy, preoccupation with being engaged at the right age "when most of the girls in the sorority were," marrying the girl who would meet the approval of an exacting, dominant mother. The list is long and varied. The consequence is, however, quite standard: awareness by middle life, and usually long before, that one has been insufficiently concerned with one's personal, psychological needs and overly concerned with career, social position, paying off parental sacrifice, and other quite honorable considerations.

It would be going too far to suggest that they have always paid for the intrusion of alien motives, or that they are aware of having done so. For some, the criteria for mate selection which others consider alien are not alien at all—they can be quite compatible with, if not the essence of, say, a passive-congenial relationship. So adequate do these criteria seem to many that they are carefully taught to their children as sensible and mature ideals by which to gear their own marital enterprises.

Trouble may and does arise, however, for those who

married for alien reasons, and who later reassess the bargain they made. A common convergence occurs by the middle years when one of the partners in such a marriage discovers that he did indeed achieve the alien purposes but that he (or she) is a much more whole person—a being whose self-expression goes beyond being an executive, or a doctor, or an artist, or a producer. It is slight comfort then to reflect that it was his own earlier choice which now limits his personal fulfillment. Such disillusionments are not ordinarily worn on the sleeve and are often thrust quickly into the unconscious. Others find it harder to dispose of the new awareness and it becomes a haunting regret.

But correct choice is not the whole story either. There is also crucial change in the mate with the passing of time. They often talked poignantly about it. A standard lament is this:

> What has become of my man? I've asked myself a thousand times. He used to be witty, conversational, a joy to be around. And now? He's self-centered, aloof, morose most of the time. His speech is dull—his very presence is flat in all dimensions. Can you tell what I mean?

It turned out this way for some of the men too:

> One of the things I'd never have dreamed possible is the way a man and a woman who married for love can within eight years become a brother and sister— respect and even a kind of love, but not an iota of anything else. First we went through the motions of sex and all that, but after a while we just got down to being like loving brother and sister. . . . Now here we

are living together, solicitous of everything that goes publicly with marriage, and everyone thinks we're really man and wife.... Can you explain this to me? We don't fight; no one is jealous; we care about what happens to one another—but isn't there something *else?*

We have deliberately said nothing about the personal histories in either of the above cases because to do so implies that we are pointing out the cause. Such feelings by middle age are, in fact, so general that we have been able to find no particular pattern which leads to this kind of outcome. Length of marriage, number of children, amount of career responsibility, and any other discernible factors appear in such variety that no pattern could be discovered which would adequately explain such change.

All change has not, of course, been destructive. Just as misalliance may evolve out of alliances which at first seemed satisfying, closeness—even love—may follow from what at first seemed to be misalliance. Some couples reported that they have "discovered each other" after several years of passive-congenial marriage—even as late as retirement, when the inexorable pressures of career and perhaps also the metabolic quiescences of later middle life provided a new perspective. Such is by no means typical, but a few have experienced it.

It's a little hard to explain, but after living together and bringing up a family and each of us going his own way, something happened. It's a little embarrassing even to have to admit, but that something includes sheer sex which I'd put out of my mind years ago and which I suspected my husband was getting somewhere else. And there's the tenderness about each other. He's interested in things about me and my world that for years he paid no attention to, and even, I suspect, thought were rather silly. So the last seven years have been a honeymoon. We still can't quite figure it out.

This is a rare sequel, but we found a few.

How widespread is misalliance? This is a question almost impossible to answer briefly and forthrightly. First, there is the conundrum of definition. Is, for example, a man mismated who says he is sure that if he had married another woman he would now be happier and more productive—but at the same time has no intention to separate or divorce? Or, again, is the husband who has denied a divorce to an outspokenly disappointed woman, mismated when he says that he is nevertheless contented with his marriage? Is the woman who is sexually cold toward her husband and carrying on a sexual affair with another man mismated if both she and her husband wish to remain married? The records on the 437 are replete with testimony clearly reflecting such enigmatic juxtapositions as these.

Faithfulness to the testimony we have gathered requires that we resist any impulse to make quantitative estimates of the incidence or degree of misalliance. Serious oversimplifications of diverse and complicated situations could easily result. Even worse, there would be a false confidence that the situation is truly understood, when in reality only a dubious statistic would have been rationalized.

More in accord with the realities of the situation and with the subtle nuances in these peoples' lives, is a summary appraisal along the two lines portrayed in this chapter: (1)

By the middle years, there is a pervasive and candid recognition among many—perhaps a third—that their mate choices had not been wise, partly because of poor initial judgment and decision and partly because of subsequent workings of the fates. (2) Radically diverse courses of action and feelings regarding these perceptions all seem to make sense, but obviously to different people. One course of action designed to rectify misalliance is divorce, the subject of the next chapter.

Chapter 5

DIVORCE

THE Significant Americans are accustomed to making decisions—often big ones. They make vital decisions at the operating table, in the courts, conference rooms, and laboratories. Their decisions shape the lives, fortunes, and destinies of the people of the nation. So when they talked about decisions in their own private worlds, they naturally tended to assume the executive stance.

A physician, forty-eight and in his second marriage, was typical when he said:

> If you think you've got a bad marriage, you have one of two choices: you get out or you stay in. It's just that simple—you make a decision. . . .

But as he went on, like others, he explained that the decision was not really so simple.

> In a way you're forever stuck with your first (and every other) mating. The residue can't be burned up

like last week's trash. It's built into too many lives—
your ex, the kids, your friends, your parents. There's
no such thing as a clear-cut set of choices. All there is
for you is the chance to choose again and maybe build
a way that holds a better hope.

Altogether we talked over more than a hundred divorce
experiences among the 437 people. The overwhelming majority of the divorced had remarried—as is the practice in all
classes in America.

Persons Experiencing Divorce

		Men	Women	Total
Divorced and Remarried		47	41	88

	(Men)	(Women)
Once	36	34
Twice or more	11	7
	47	41

	Men	Women	Total
Divorced and Not Remarried	10	7	17
	57	48	105

24% (105/437)

Of the seventeen people interviewed who had not as yet remarried, about half intended to. Another fifty of the 437
interviewees said that they had considered divorce, but thus
far had not actually taken the final step.

+50

=36%

We found practically no evidence of impulsive decisions
to seek divorce. The overwhelming impression is the reverse;
when divorce occurred in these people's lives, it typically
came as an "end of the rope" decision after a period of three
or four or even as long as ten or twelve years of awareness—
usually mutual—that the marriage was unsatisfactory.

You just put it off and put it off. . . . By hindsight
I have wondered why. The state of wanting to and yet
not doing it, though, isn't always the hell that it is
some of the time. My friends who have been through
the mill mostly agree with me—you keep hoping and
no one knows what for. . . .

Quite often the dissolution of the "state of suspension,"
which characterizes so many misallied couples' lives together
was triggered by the appearance of the "engaging alternative." It's an old story, but we heard it over and over from
men and from women:

I know it makes me sound immature or like I
didn't respect my age (fifty-three) but all of a sudden—
really, it wasn't so sudden—I began to yearn for the
kind of life I had briefly in the early years of my first
marriage. Very probably though the balance was
tipped when I got to know Jean. That really reminded
me of what I had stamped out of my life over the
years. . . . We were just friendly at first. She worked at
the office beyond the call of duty—and not for any
favors. I found myself sharing all sorts of thoughts and
ideas with her—and—oh hell, you must have heard all
this before. I know so many cases—and I haven't even
made a study of it. . . . Anyway, we tried it as an affair
for a while and the nearer we got to playing husband
and wife, the more we wanted it for real. I paid pretty
dearly for it—as the world sees prices—but it's the best
investment I ever made. If there's anything I'm bitter
about, it's those long wasted years. . . . You can under-

stand why "September Song" isn't just another set of lyrics for me.

No other single reason was mentioned as frequently as finding a mate who seemed better to fit the man's or the woman's needs and wants—an engaging alternative to the lackluster of one's present circumstances. Almost all of them said that they maintained pretenses for public consumption, but that the real decision came in this way.

Generally, both of a pair do not find someone else at the same time, or even feel a desire for another spouse. In these cases, as might be expected, the decision to go along with a mate's desire to be free is not an easy one. The initial response is often like this editor's. At forty-five he thought he could keep the situation under control—for himself at least:

> Why should I let her go? We don't fight much— probably no worse than most married couples. She's a good mother. She doesn't refuse me sex, even though I know she's really gone on the other guy. She has no grounds against *me*.

But in time he did go along—and rather soon at that. In a later interview he said:

> What else was there to do? It's no fun, by god, to sleep with a woman who'd rather have someone else— and does every time she can scheme it out. I began to feel like a prison warden or slave keeper or something. . . . We started getting sharper and sharper with each other—and the kids noticed it, too. . . . And when you get down to it, it's damned humiliating to be upstaged like that.

The reluctant-divorced, then, usually in the end go along with the request of a spouse to terminate a marriage. There are women who even initiate the termination because under the circumstances they are "too outraged to do anything else." But they did not want the divorce in the first place—they found the marriage to be at least minimally adequate. Others had to be "manipulated and maneuvered" into divorce by the spouse who wanted out.

We found, however, that as a rule by the time a divorce is legally formalized, both of the spouses desire to have the marriage terminated, even though earlier, one was more clearly the aggressor. There seems to be a recognition among some of them:

> A satisfying relationship is a two-way thing. Except in the most rare circumstances, and for the most insensitive people, contentment for *one* is difficult if not impossible, unless there is a reciprocating sentiment on the part of the other.

Both men and women expressed this philosophy to us.

The divorced among the subjects of our study are a heterogeneous group, then, as seen in terms of their motivations, their emotions, and their life styles. Outside of the standard legal designation, they have exceedingly little in common. Important distinctions stand out.

Much emotionally charged writing, both in fiction and in serious scientific work, has depicted the broken, embittered, hostile, divorced person as if this were a preponderant type. Divorce is presented as a great personal tragedy leaving a burdensome and often unmanageable emotional residue.

Sometimes, of course, we did find such instances. But there are many other types. There is also the relieved person, one for whom the dissolved marriage was, by the time of the divorce or long before, so seriously frustrating that to have gotten out of it was to have shed an unbearable burden. Such a freed person sometimes looks forward eagerly to a new existence, the beckon of which is deeply sustaining.

Most of the divorced, it must be remembered, are transient. Seven out of eight divorced people in the United States remarry, usually quite soon. After thirty years of age, as reported by a Metropolitan Life Insurance Study, chances of marriage for a divorced woman are two to five times greater than for a never-married woman of corresponding age. For most of the people we talked to, divorce was a required legal preliminary to a new marriage, very often a mere legitimation of a psychological *fait accompli*. As a psychiatrist told us:

> Almost all divorcees are belatedly getting out of a situation which has long been psychologically detrimental. They seem to wait and wait until someone takes them by the hand and leads them out.

The transient-divorced have problems too, but these are largely practical ones, such as carrying out of the property and custody arrangements, residential change to meet legal requirements, and sometimes a change in job or locale. But they are problems which, however awkward and emotionally draining, are usually resolved by these people through some adroit, expedient solution. The people work them out as best they can in an atmosphere of hope and security derived from their new orientation—"It's a matter of cleaning it up."

The divorced vary also with respect to their relationships

with the former mate. In some instances there is little but open hostility; every opportunity is used to inflict penalty, bring recrimination or harm on the former spouse. This is sometimes accomplished with a candor and an effectiveness which are impressive:

> When he told me he was in love with another woman and moved out and asked for a divorce, I simply told the children (six years to fifteen) that their father didn't love them any more either, or he wouldn't do this to them. We are all one unit—the children and me—if he leaves me, he leaves them. I didn't forbid them to see him, but I made it clear that I didn't *expect* them to see him either, even though he does have legal visitation rights. My oldest girl ran into him at the village and refused to speak to him. Kids understand a lot, you know. . . . I got a very good settlement and alimony. . . . I don't really need it, you know. My law practice is almost as good as his. . . .

In sharp contrast there is a considerable proportion of divorces in which the former mates remain friendly and cooperative. A woman executive typifies those who worked it out this way:

> My former husband and I see each other a great deal and remain quite friendly. Actually, come to think of it, we're more genuinely and honestly friendly than when we were married. In some ways, if you have children, you never get a complete divorce. You have to talk together to plan any number of things concerning the kids—but even if you didn't have the kids, you

would. When I see him or he calls, we chat at length about things we've read, political events, things that happen to our mutual friends—just about everything outside of the intimate subjects that any married couple might. Why not? . . . My fiancé sometimes drops in with me when I have some business with my former husband and we often all have a drink together. (This is four years after the divorce.) After all, we're all civilized people. He *is* the father of my children, you know. Besides he probably suffered as much in the marriage as I did—maybe more.

. . . We still both have the same circle of friends as we did before and occasionally we run into each other at social functions. Nobody seems to mind, since we obviously get along fine.

Another way of sorting them out is to look at the divorced —or as we did, allow them to look at themselves—"a little later." Again, some types are identifiable. There are the successfully divorced, those who found through divorce a way to a better life. They look back upon the experience, however harrowing at the time, with the conviction that they are better off now. The defeated-divorced, on the other hand, have a different hindsight. If they were once hopeful that the divorce was a way to another life, for one reason or another that hope has been shattered.

I divorced him to be free to marry Chet, to start over again, as we often used to say to each other. Well, when my divorce was final, Chet started to cool off. I guess the earlier intrigue was what he wanted, not me. . . . So now I'm alone. The pickings, even for flings, aren't much. . . . It's all a mess.

Some never hoped at all. And a few consider it unrealistic to do so. A few—very few—still carry the torch, as this man does, after five years:

I went along with the divorce idea—what can you do? You don't *own* a woman. But I knew then, and still do, that it was the end of what I was really living for.

Between the clearly successful and the clearly defeated is an ambivalent group. They feel no consistent or clear valences, either way. They vary from mood to mood, and "from stab to stab" at working out a satisfying life pattern. Some stay this way indefinitely. Others move in the direction of facing up one way or another, and then either join the ranks of the successful or admit defeat.

These are all recurring types. Divorced people, like married ones, are found to be of diverse kinds when viewed totally, empathically, and objectively. Another interpretation, based on a few simplitudes about human nature and a pervasive moralism, would, of course, see it otherwise.

The Significant Americans, like others, seem to be confused in their philosophies about divorce. In the abstract there is mostly an easy-going tolerance—"It's everybody's own business." But in the actual situation, tolerance sometimes comes a little harder. Part of their reluctance, they said, is simply the threat to established habit. Friends who become divorced introduce vexing problems into social relations. Divorced persons, largely because of long established stereo-

types, may introduce awkwardness into entertainment
protocol. And even if they don't, their mere presence constitutes an all too vivid reminder of the impermanence of
the male-female relationship. Nevertheless, people in this
class have been widely and often intimately exposed to
divorce. While not exactly casual, they tend to be empathic
to the intentions of divorced persons and amoral about the
process. We found little moral preachment concerning "the
institution of marriage," although among insecure and
socially upgraded wives there is a general uneasiness lest
divorce catch up with them. This woman, a self-styled "plain
Jane" whose life she says is centered in her children, spoke
for several others:

> Every time someone at the office or in the neighbor-
> hood gets divorced, I get so mad I could scream. You
> wonder when it will hit you. I know I'm no prize pack-
> age for Jim—compared to the women he's around all
> the time. He says he loves me, but we both know I
> don't really fit with his family and all. He keeps telling
> about how well off we are with three fine kids and
> all. . . . Sometimes I think he's whistling in the dark,
> you know. . . .

But there is also a widespread recognition among those
we spoke to that a divorce may be therapeutic. An internist
commented with evident feeling based on long professional
experience concerning the reluctance of many to use divorce
as a bid for a better life:

> In my experience I would have to say that there
> are more people acting unwisely, doing themselves

serious damage, and exerting a bad influence on the community by trying to perpetuate dying or dead relationships than there are those who are able to recognize, however tardily, that it's time for a change. . . . By the way, the analogy to physical medicine is rather striking. Just as I can prolong life for my patients sometimes many, many weeks through the administration of drugs, so people with dying relationships on their hands prolong them for months and years, chiefly through the medicinal properties of alcohol. And in place of transfusions they get all kinds of temporary lifts by trying expediencies on the rare chance that they might possibly work some miracle, though good sense should indicate it highly unlikely.

The rebuttal, if it is one, is found in the testimony of those who refuse to "rock the boat," and admonish others to "stick it out." There is a very strong accent—verbal and actual—on marital permanence, almost regardless of the psychic cost. Such people freely acknowledge that their marriages are in one or more ways seriously disappointing, possibly because they made unfortunate choices or because times and tides have carried them far afloat from the promising isles they knew earlier. They know, factually, that some people in similar circumstances have used the escape hatch of divorce, tried a second launching, and often found a new and better isle that way. But the "price seems too high," all costs considered, and it seems better, therefore, to make less drastic adaptations—or simply to do nothing at all.

Those who do not want to rock the boat are not to be considered as a type. They are a "motivational category"—

they are merely people who try so to organize and redirect their lives as to countervail this one set of frustrations. They hold themselves on tight rein, while often candidly acknowledging that they would prefer to be free. One device is simply to devalue "the male-female stuff" in comparison to other life matters. So they place the man-woman relationship, one way or another, on the fringe of importance. They feel they have cogent reasons for this choice (as do also those who choose otherwise). This reasoning is remarkably standard. This business executive spoke for a large group when he said:

> What you do when you finally face up to the fact that life just doesn't hold for you the kind of private excitement and reassurance and deep personal reward that it does for other people—you just have to make a choice. . . . My first impulse was to chuck it all and start over again. But the disenchantment isn't quite that dramatic and the longer I thought about it, the clearer the alternatives seemed to me. It's like making a major adjustment in the business. The choices aren't quite black and white and so you try to work out the best course of action, on balance. On one side of the ledger are the kids, who so far as I can see are not aware that their mother and I are now husband and wife in name only. Well, that's not exactly right either —I mean, damn it, we don't sleep together—except now and then when we get plastered or sentimental or it's an anniversary. Since we don't fight and we really sort of like each other, I think the kids assume that they have an ordinary father and mother. Of

course, they don't see any affection either, but I don't suppose most kids do....

Then there's my wife—a pretty decent gal any way you look at her—well, not *any* way—she's really kind of dull, she's preoccupied with her menopause and being a good wife and all that. But the point is, she isn't mean—you should hear some of the female bitching I've heard after a couple of rounds of drinks at just about any cocktail party.... And then, of course, there's the business, which is half hers, not just legally but by rights. Shortly after we were married, her father took me in and by the time he died, I was the co-owner. I don't know how in hell you could work out a decent legal settlement.

So, you see, I still have the comforts of home like other guys. Of course, I do like a piece now and then —less often now. But there are enough trips and other opportunities around here. It just all sort of adds up that it's sometimes better to make your peace with things as they are.

Another group consists of couples who say that they are going to get a divorce "some day."

It's a hell of a way to live—this way—we're both full of regrets and hurts and suspicions—and pretty well-founded ones too. We go our own ways in all the important things—even sex—except that she doesn't get much any more. I don't even know if she wants to any more. She just runs a very efficient and attractive house —I can't quite say "home" any more—and she's good with the kids. We've talked it all over and decided that when Dick (the youngest) gets into college, we'll do it. That's a good time, you know, because a kid is really weaned from home when he leaves for college— from then on it's just weekend visiting and a vacation, if you're lucky. (Dick is now twelve; his father is forty-eight.)

Many couples like this say that they loathe the interim period, yet they find one reason after another for not rocking the boat "at this time"—later on, "the children will be older; they'll understand better," or "after I've worked out a better financial arrangement," or "when I'm more sure of my position," or "when I'm sure I can get away with it." But so often these times just never seem to come. The children do get older but the couple still doubt their "understanding." No workable financial arrangement ever seems quite suitable. And many are never sure enough of their positions that they judge they can "get away with it." And so they continue, not rocking the boat now but holding to the dream that some day they may. And perhaps some day, faced with an "engaging alternative'" they will, but in the absence of one, it is clear that they will continue in the not-too-uncomfortable routine.

Some of those who prefer not to rock the boat gave us some conceptions of love which further reinforce their middle-life choice of "sticking it out." Most of their marriages, they said, started in a mood which they identified as love. Despite the tragic inroads on these early sentiments brought about by growings-away, by the residues from overt and unconscious conflict, by hurt from the desertions and disillusions which accumulate, often something of the original feeling endures. They say that they "still love" or "sort of love" or "think they love" the grown-away-from spouse. Less often, but still significantly, there are those who frankly say that they love their spouses more than anyone else, but not enough to limit their companionship and sex behavior in accordance therewith.

Thus, one man who has not shared a bed with his wife for twenty-five years and lives away from her almost all of the time—meanwhile having a common-law marriage with another woman with whom he has had a child—insists that he would resist a divorce even if his wife wanted it, because he "still loves" her. This kind of assertion, though usually not so clearly contradicted by the facts, is not really unique.

As they conversed about love—and by no means all of them did—they presented some typical images which would give the semanticist a bad time. Whatever the word stood for at first, by the middle years it has become synonymous with pity for some, simple acceptance of responsibility for others, the need to repay a debt for still others.

There's nothing to do but love a half-invalid woman who you know has given the best and only whole years of herself to a mutual enterprise. We've bred and borne children together, been through dreadful anguish and sheer fright together. . . . She's like my right hand, or something else that I can't quite imagine life without. . . . She's so helpless and pitiful. . . . When I go away on business trips or vacations, I realize that this is all a sentimental attachment to something of years ago and I know very well that before she got ill we were estranged and lived independent lives and were both adulterous. . . . And we've never been reconciled either.

And another:

Oh, I know he's fat, grouchy, and not romantic any more. Sometimes he's even mean and I know he's often been unfaithful. Yet the small part of the time when he's here is fuller than the rest. I'd miss him if he stayed away altogether. I supposed that's what love *is* by the fifties.

So they go on, substantial numbers of them, inexorably moving away from each other in vital matters. Yet they cling to the life jackets of tradition, to gentler memories, and to a useful practical life arrangement, zestlessly and ritual- istically playing out the days. A few openly admitted that they are waiting for an "act of God" to free them.

Whatever may be the full range of theoretical alternatives which might logically follow acknowledged mismating, the people whom we interviewed have tried each of the two obvi- ous paths. Some stick it out—one way or another. Others divorce or separate. The division isn't equal. The clear majority *intend* to stick it out—by choice or by drift. They don't always succeed; if not, they eventually resort to divorce anyway. But as a whole, the alternative of "doing nothing drastic about it" fits the larger life perspectives of many Upper-Middle-Class people quite well. Their important areas of commitment are often outside of male-female interests anyway and they are reinforced in such commitments by other like-minded people. Practical considerations, and even some emotional ones like children and home, also help to sustain them in their determined intention to stick it out.

And so they argue among themselves and strive for clear and consistent views as to whether divorce is a good or a bad thing and when and by whom it ought to be used. The Significant Americans, like others, tend to have a double standard about it—in the abstract they are tolerant, even though they do not consistently see divorce in positive terms, that is, as a sound social policy and as a rational personal device. Part of the ambivalence seems to be related to personal experience: had divorce occurred in the lives of people with whom one had been really close? How did it work out for them? Is divorce a threat to oneself now? And, if so, is one the aggressor or the reluctant party? All this and other involvements make a clear difference as to how they see the question. And, it should be said, those with the most dogmatic, unequivocal views, either way, were people with the least direct exposure to the divorce process.

Chapter 6

UTILITARIAN MARRIAGE

A LARGE proportion of the Significant Americans live in a diffuse marital arrangement which, they explained so often, they consider to be rational and satisfying. Their justification for it is simply that it works well for them. It is a life style which enables them to meet their demanding career obligations effectively; it meliorates many of the potentially disturbing effects of widespread mismating, and it meets the monolithic societal expectations which many of them hesitate to offend. That many of its features run counter to the judgments and sentiments of some of their associates is to be expected, in view of the present varied climate of opinion regarding men, women, sex, marriage, and parenthood.

One woman described a common marital evolution. She told first of a period of early marriage during which she and her husband enjoyed a full and vital relationship. Then a slow erosion wore away one after another of the ties which provided the ecstasy for those first few years. Rather suddenly she became aware of the radically different way they were living.

> ... At thirty-eight you're not *old,* yet you find that sex has gotten humdrum, the children fill your time with trivia—no stimulation, just fatigue. You hardly ever see your husband and when you do, he's preoccupied with other things. These all creep up on you and all of a sudden you realize you're *never* going to be a couple again—not really!
>
> When it first hit me, I was all shook up, as the kids say. I cried and blabbed to my brother—cried over the phone about it even. ... But I got a perspective about it after a while—and it really wasn't anything so new— I knew it all along. I just couldn't give up. ... That was six years ago. ...
>
> Now we have it worked out perfectly. He travels— the whole southwest now that he's been promoted— and only gets home alternate weekends. And I teach —well, really, I'm the principal in a pretty exclusive girls' school. We've moved to the country now and Joey can have his horses and Ellen has her boating and swimming close by.
>
> At first it seemed like such a compromise—and I did consider a divorce, but that's foolish—you just get into the same bind again.
>
> Anyway, there's a lot of nothing between me and Bob—we might as well face it. When he comes home it's exciting at first but after a while. ... Really, there's no sentiment or closeness there. I don't know whether he's got someone or something on the road—but what's

the difference? I'm not losing anything. And he's had to forgive (or anyway not divorce me over) an affair or two. So you just balance it out.

Anyway, we've worked it all out—equally and fairly. When we go to visit our families in the summer, we spend half of the time with each set of grandparents—minus the time for travel. We work it out as exactly as we can. We both want to be *fair* about everything.

And we have our beautiful new home now. The children have their own rooms. And I have my new car—only mine is a hardtop. Bob likes a sports coupe —but that floor shift is a nuisance. . . .

Another route to a similar outcome is explained by an executive who was rather clear about his original motivations:

I can tell you why *I* got married! I was getting to the place where I had to. I'd gone up in the corporation as far as I could as a single man. Why they're so prejudiced in favor of married men, I'll never know. Maybe it's those psychological adjustment guys in Personnel. Anyway, I wanted Carl's job so bad I could taste it and I knew he was moving on in a year or so. So I looked around. None of the gals I was sleeping with quite filled the bill. So I looked around some more. And then I lit on Charmaine. Now I know it's sort of a "married the boss' daughter" routine, but really it's not quite so bad. She wanted to join up with a marriage as bad as I did. She'd had enough of this career stuff and she was ready for maternity wards and rose gardens. So we did it. . . .

Now we've got ten years' perspective on it and three kids. . . .

But neither of us has welshed on the bargain. We stay out of each other's lives all we can, but we cooperate in every way with what the other one wants. She's been a sweety about it—and I don't think I've let her down either. I told her before we were married that she could have fifty per cent of my income after taxes to run the house and spend on herself and no questions asked. And the rest was mine and no questions asked. We leave each other's private lives alone —and not because either of us has anything to hide— it's just a principle. . . .

Now *don't* ask me if I love her, or if she loves me. That doesn't mean anything anyway. We have fun together if we don't see too much of each other. I'm kind of proud of her—a dish, really, for her age. And I know she's proud as hell to be married to the executive vice-president. That ought to be enough for anybody!

By the term Utilitarian Marriage we mean simply any marriage which is established or maintained for purposes other than to express an intimate, highly important *personal* relationship between a man and a woman. The absence of continuous and deep empathic feeling and the existence of an atmosphere of limited companionship are natural outcomes, since the purposes for its establishment or maintenance are not primarily sexual and emotional ones. Hence the term *utilitarian;* the marriage is useful to the mates for reasons outside of personal considerations.

It is, however, an "institutional form," as sociologists like to put it, which fulfills important wants and needs. It is made-to-order for pairs who have evolved conflict-habituated, devitalized, or passive-congenial relationships. Whatever the differences among these three, there is a common element: "male-female stuff," joyful sex, close companionship, deep emotional involvement, are not of major importance and are only occasionally present. The cohesive forces which maintain the union come out of other purposes and provide other kinds of satisfactions. This marital institution, nevertheless, makes a good deal of sense to many Significant Americans.

The "alien motives" for marriage which were discussed in Chapter 4 explain how some people, like the man just quoted, first find their way into a Utilitarian Marriage. Prestigeful occupation, high education attainment, "promise," "good family," and such are indisputably desirable attributes to have in a spouse—particularly for the men and women in the group we studied. Moreover, since marriage also may provide entree to such important enhancements of success as "contacts" and "connections," if not an actual position in an established business or professional partnership, often a more compelling seduction than that prompted by love takes place.

It doesn't seem to them, as a rule, quite so cold-blooded, however. An engineer, at fifty-three, recalled the process in cool, passive-congenial terms:

When you're young it's *easy* to be in love, or as we older people like to say, to *think* you are in love. Girls are fun to be around; sex is still new. Most of us dated a good deal and took on two notions which by

middle life a lot of us now question. One I would call
the interchangeability of women, because when you're
young, you know, they really are. And the other is the
idea that sex is sort of automatic—you can always count
on it. What I mean is that rare is the youngster who
has any real understanding of the infinite possibilities
of good sex as the middle-aged person can know it.
Nobody could have told me this at the time, but I
know it now. . . . So, you see, whether I was in love or
just thought I was doesn't make much difference. . . .
It was some years before I realized that what was
really attractive about her was her father's position in
my profession and her ease in associating with the
kind of people I wanted to associate with. Pedigree
again.

Such considerations, whether conscious or not, seem to be
sensible and rational to the people in this class, as we have
so often seen.

That tricky countercurrents arise for some of them is
hardly surprising. Even though certain extrinsic attributes
of a woman may be helpful to a man's success and social
acceptance, they may not be the ones which will make her
a scintillating, empathic female companion for him over the
years. Nevertheless, typically the men try to see the more
positive side of the later realization. "But she's such a good
mother," or "She contributed a lot to my success" are phrases
which they use repeatedly, as if to tell us (and also to reassure
themselves) that the present loneliness they feel is a price
they paid, and they are still trying to be good sports about it.
The women's stock lines are only a little different. "He's

given me and the children everything we could want," or "He's worked so hard for us," or "I'm so proud of him," or "This community owes him a lot."

Most Utilitarian Marriages emerge slowly as new life requirements and opportunities unfold. Typically they are not formed at first, although some pairs settled in almost as soon as the honeymoon was over. Usually it took longer—at least to the birth of the second or third child. A sensitive, poetic woman who had become a free-lance writer during her late thirties explained complacently, if a little ruefully, that one can settle for "rather little spousal living," after a while.

> When you're young—in college, and until after the first baby—you don't realize how much adaptation (isn't that the word?) you will willingly make. . . . Here I am, a very young (and I'm told still attractive) grandmother, plenty of money, good health, free to do what I wish, and I just stay here at home and read and write a little. . . . We've had separate bedrooms since my first pregnancy over twenty-five years ago. . . . But we are not estranged. The door to my room is never closed and a few times a year it is darkened by his shadow in the night.

This woman offered no hint that she felt seriously mismated, much less resentful. Like many others, she has come to accept a life of quite modest fulfillments so far as spousal intimacy is concerned. Women in this circumstance give at least a superficial impression of contentment which often persists even after the longer and deeper look is completed.

One of these women says she is comforted and reassured

when her husband tells her, for example, how much her services are missed when she has to be temporarily away from home. Men are not, as a rule, stingy with compliments in this department. The following account gave the wife evident pleasure.

> So I took the kids on a little weekend trip like we go on almost every week—but this was while Pat was visiting her mother. Well it was a debacle—from start to finish. I had no idea how much planning and how many separate arrangements it took to get that show on the road. Never again—unless she's here to manage it. . . . It's easier to take a regiment on a six month encampment. . . . You've just got to have a woman around.

Yet she is no mere workhorse. The wife of a Significant American is free from the meaner kinds of poverty and is quite free to indulge herself in various ways. This she accomplishes by drinking with impunity, having her own car and exercising some measure of personal expression in overseeing the civic institutions of the community. Since her husband is likely to be an organization man, some considerable effort goes into facilitation of his movement up the escalator of the bureaucracy. But the central valence in all this is the quiet, confident knowledge that this is mainly what a good wife ought to do, and she wants to do it. Her children and her home occupy her time and energies, and provide her expressive fulfillments. Some husbands cooperate so fully in the parental tasks that such activities completely express the couples' personal lives. Children often loom large in the values of these people, sometimes to the virtual exclusion of everything else. For instance, the following account:

> The only important thing in our life is the children. Max gave up a pretty good promotion because it would have meant moving and we want to stay here because the boys are doing so beautifully in school. We don't want to uproot them. Our youngest is very shy and it would be hard on him. Why, even when he wanted to learn to play the saxophone so much, he just couldn't make himself do it alone. You know, I actually took lessons with him for a year to get him started. And now this year my husband is managing the Little League team and Jim (the middle son) is catcher. He'd hate to leave the team now. He and his daddy are quite a pair. I've never seen a father and son so devoted to each other. I don't think we belong to a single organization that doesn't have to do with the welfare of the kids—Church, Scouts, Little League, the Swim Club— we're really a family. Our oldest boy even comes home from college every other weekend and we all go up to see him the weekends that he doesn't make the trip. There's something special to a mother about her first-born. We're all very close.

Meanwhile, she succeeds in staying as young as her health and modern cosmetology will allow. She is other-directed, cheery, and chatty, knows what is going on in the world— but not too much about it—has no serious doubts about the future so long as "people have good will and a decent respect for the amenities." All in all, whether she admits it or not in so many words, she is a **functional** adjunct to **a largely** asexual world (for her) and is contentedly conscientious about her importance in fashioning the next generation of it.

But by no means all wives are absorbed in the traditional home-and-family enterprise. Almost a third of the wives with whom we talked are career women. Sometimes they follow careers far afield from those of their husbands, and even if they are in the same profession, they may prefer to operate quite independently. They have the same need as do men, however, for a home base not only for personal convenience but also to facilitate their careers. They often have had their children early in life and are able to employ parent-substitutes of high quality to take over the home while they are busy. These women function essentially as men do in the society and find marriage convenient as a background for their busy professional lives. They enjoy "having it both ways"—an exciting career plus the more conventional comforts of home.

Still others simply prefer an existence which allows them a degree of freedom and independence but still gives them the stability of home and family. Some, like this woman, seem very content with peripheral spousehood.

> The key to our marriage is respect. We really respect each other's individuality. I don't smother him and he doesn't smother me. The only time we really had any trouble was when he first started the business. He made home his office and I nearly went crazy with him underfoot. These gals that wish they could share in their husband's work can have it! I'd been in the laboratory with him before we got married, but when he was home all the time and I had other things to do,

it was a different story, I can tell you! Now it's perfect. He's on the road a little more than half the time and when he's been gone a week or so I really miss him and look forward to seeing him again. We have one hell of a reunion! Then after he's home four or five days, we're starting to get on each other's nerves again. But mostly when he's here I have a wonderful time with him. And when he's gone I have a wonderful time with others. I'm happy either way.

She went on to speak enthusiastically about concerts and bridge parties she attends with mixed groups while her husband is gone, assuring us that her husband knows of these things and does not object. "Since he doesn't like either concerts or bridge, he doesn't feel he's missing much." She also assumes that her husband has his own activities while he's on the road and feels that he is entitled to his own privacy in the matter. She added, "Knowing him, he's probably got his nose in a book the whole time."

For many men, too, the Utilitarian Marriage is tailor-made. The Upper-Middle-Class man never quite escapes, or often wants to, the career centrality of his life. Careers are demanding—physically, psychologically, and in practically every other way. Yet the career man is, with few exceptions, expected also to be a "family man." As a rule he doesn't need much urging, because he wants this too. The Utilitarian Marriage maximizes his occasional need for freedom—freedom to travel extensively, freedom

. . . to avoid if I can, too much time with my wife. She's that oppressive kind of woman; she always wants

to hang around and is always looking for a smooch.
It's too distracting.

He went on to reassure us that he thought himself quite
normal, however:

> I like a woman as much as any man, but only once
> in a while, and when *I* want her.

To many career men the home is almost an adjunct to
the job. It is not simply that he needs it as a place to enter-
tain—although this can be important. It is a status symbol, at
once evidence of his past successes and a recommendation to
support his bid for more. The organization man in many
corporations and in some of the independent professions says
that he is practically required to maintain a "certain kind"
of home. He often has to trade on his home and family as he
does on his personality. "It's all part of a package which you
present to your public."

Running through his imagery and his dependence upon
home and family are the related concepts of stability and security. When some of these men talk about home and family
they suggest an image of a feudal manor house: it is a place
of protection, a base from which the expedition moves out
and to which it returns for replenishment. If this seems vague
and sentimental, it is because many of these men themselves
are so. The only uneasiness they have about this way of life
relates to concerns about how to strengthen, stabilize, pro-
tect, or adorn the manor.

For some men, of course, there is need for a special security
which home and family also provide. These are the men who
candidly admit that they fulfill their erotic needs, whether

for the "furtive catch-as-catch-can escapade" or for the more enduring and fulfilling total companionship outside of marriage. While there is always some risk of exposure, and wives may or may not be cooperative about it, this method of having one's cake and eating it is by no means true. If his mistress changes her mind when she understands that she is really only on the fringe of importance to him and that he is still playing the role of the stable family man, she may transfer her affections or refuse to go along with his occasional visits to her. When these discouragements occur, the man can return to home base to lick his wounds before the next adventure.

By no means all of the men who acknowledge extramarital affairs are so cynical about it. Some are men of deep compassion and often are torn between commitments to their children (and even to their wives) and their impelling desires for other deep personal expression. Sometimes the conflict is simply between the necessity of maintaining a public appearance of a happy marriage and the need for a more intensely emotional life. This is typically the case when a divorce would seriously jeopardize the man's career.

A further general reinforcement supports the Utilitarian Marriage, however; sincere ideological commitment to what we have earlier called the monolithic code. Despite contrary overt behaviors, many of these men and women hold to self-images which are quite moral. They accept the stable, affluent socially correct Utilitarian Marriage as a natural and inevitable base of operations, and they have "appropriate sentiments" about it.

For some, there are additional reinforcements which they explained to us too. There are people in the Upper Middle

Class, as elsewhere, who have little capacity for sexual expression and little interest in the opposite sex. These people are not necessarily hostile, but they are aloof, "can take it or leave it," usually have little sex need, and are not in the least romantic about anything personal. Yet they like the comforts of home, wish to have children and desire to be seen as quite normal by their peers. Provided they can find or fashion a mate of similar views and needs—or one who will make and keep a bargain of this sort—the Utilitarian Marriage is a happy solution.

Then, too, there are the devitalized pairs, the couples who, despite the accumulated disappointments, still prefer to remain married for the well-known practical and moral reasons. Yet they know—although sometimes only one has faced up to it—that there is no real marriage any more in the sense that there formerly was.

For others, the Utilitarian Marriage is simply a good ad interim arrangement, until such time as they judge they can see their way clear to a divorce. They differ from the foregoing people in that they consciously intend "when Shirley starts college" or "when Bob gets the Denver territory" or "when Jim's Fulbright to Ghana comes through" to make the open break. "In the meantime two reasonable adults have to work out *something* to carry them on without too much emotional mayhem."

Thus, regardless of whether the man wants or needs to escape from home and family, or wants to keep it on the periphery of his interests and physical regimen, or wishes to be closely identified with it, the Utilitarian Marriage works. If he wants to go to Europe for a year or slip off for a weekend at the Mardi Gras with his girl, he is free to go without much anxiety. The "operation" will go on efficiently while he is away. Yet, if he's running for office or seeking an important position, he can invite the cameras in, throw open the doors, parade his children and his comely and proper wife for all to admire. And if he merely needs a quiet, undemanding private life in order to pursue his important and very demanding career life, the Utilitarian Marriage is the solution. This in fact is frequently what they mean when they speak of "comforts of home and family" in the Utilitarian Marriage.

And yet the Utilitarian Marriage is decidedly inconvenient for some. Some men and women say they feel too vital and "too honest" to yield more than half-heartedly and temporarily to this admittedly practical but emotionally neutral arrangement. They are repelled by an apathetic marriage; they feel cheated. They refuse to accept the cliché that sex is mostly for the young, and the women assert that they do not in fact find their chief sex expression in the bearing and rearing of their children, "as some of the more articulate eunuchs of our society would have us believe."

As these women explained the progression of their entrapment in the Utilitarian Marriage, they recalled flashes of insight which brought the true, and resented, picture into focus for them:

> When my father had his heart attack, I went home to be with him. Busy and worried as I was, I missed my husband. I was really lonely for him. When I came back, George told me how he'd missed me and how he never really appreciated me before. I thought he was

going to throw me into bed and make me see stars! But he only meant the more practical things. I guess the kids were pretty whiney while I was gone and he's a mess at managing things. He had a list a mile long of things that had gone wrong while I was away. Even so, I didn't really catch on. It wasn't until just this past summer that it finally dawned on me. I thought he'd enjoy taking the boys on a camping trip and really roughing it a little—just him and the three kids. He didn't go for the idea at all—he said it didn't sound like much fun to him to cook over a smoky fire and have pans to clean out and gear to keep in order and three fighting kids to separate besides. You know what he said to me? "If you'd go along, it would be O.K." That's what he said. So now I know. I'm just part of the camping equipment.

Yet there are usually stabilizing considerations—and they can loom important too, provided they can sustain her. The same woman went on to say:

But I feel like a heel complaining about him. He's never late coming home; he never gets drunk; he doesn't gamble his money away; he doesn't chase around. I guess I should be satisfied, shouldn't I? But darn it, I'm not—I want to see stars at least *once* in a while.

Men don't necessarily like the Utilitarian Marriage any better than do their women.

I've often asked myself one question during these last few years: Is *this* what it's all for? I maintain a

home—an elegant one—which takes about all I can
wring out of the business. It often takes *everything*.
I've got to do it too. Marge manages the house and
brings up the kids—and we meet alone now and then
—well, we meet once or twice a month in bed. And
even then, it's pretty flat and routine. We try to spice
it up with a little booze and some sexy talk, but hell!
it's like putting air into a tire with a hole in it—nothing happens. Even a fight would be a relief—at least
there'd be some excitement—somebody would at least
want to win.

The Significant Americans, as a rule, don't give up easily.
They are accustomed to handling stubborn problems and
most of them are where they are because they are adroit at
managing human affairs. They naturally turn to this com-
petency when problems arise at home. First, as this commercial artist explained, there is the stage of growing awareness.

. . . nothing dramatic, just a slow recognition that
we didn't have much in common that we both *really*
cared about. And a few things were clearly irritating
besides. I wasn't very fancy in bed—enough vigor I
guess but little finesse—all those college girls didn't
really teach me a damn thing. My wife wasn't too
smart about it either, but she did know enough to
realize, I guess, that we were missing something that
she thought was important. . . . It wasn't only sex that
we got crossed up about. Whenever we got to talking,
we always—well, not really always, but often enough
that we couldn't miss it—we would very quickly get

to the point where there was nothing to talk about any more. We just sat and looked at each other. . . .

Then he explained with pride how they fashioned a form of adaptation which many resort to with confidence and which does yield a certain kind of success.

We worked out a *system*—it wasn't really so formal as a system but at least it was a course of action. It took the sting out of it for us. It took the hurt out. To avoid running out of interesting conversation, we just stopped trying to start serious talk at all. We cultivated our own separate interests and even separate friends. It's really surprising how many things you can find to do right here in this community that don't involve a couple. Why, even in our church . . .

We call this kind of solution an Avoidance Device. It is rooted in the folk wisdom which holds that problems can be solved, or at least their adverse effects avoided or countervailed, by devoting effort and attention to something else.

Practically any activity may become for someone a way of avoiding a frustrating marital situation. People with substandard marriages are typically advised by friends, or figure out for themselves, that having a baby, or another one, buying a house in the country, going back to school, cultivating new interests, joining a church, or serving as a Scout Master "will cure what ails you."

In a sense it does. The new activity takes time—and energy. Since both are finite, any sustained attention to a substitute activity may be expected to reduce the opportunities for irritation. One highly successful woman attorney explained in an early interview:

> I don't have much of a sex life, but I have come to realize that there are other things in life besides sex. . . . My husband and I very seldom go out together and we don't do any entertaining any more—he doesn't like my friends, and he doesn't even want his in. He thinks practically all women are stupid—and says so. . . . My children occupy me quite a bit; I have a housekeeper so I'm free to go to lectures or concerts alone or with a girl friend and I have time to dabble in some more education. . . . I don't think much about sex any more. I think more about other things and I form my important associations with people interested in the same kinds of things.

In other words, the absence of a vital spousal relationship is sensibly compensated for by asserting that vitality and closeness between mates are not really important, and then substituting something else to take their place.

In fact, avoidance devices of one sort or another are employed by so many that they have taken on an almost institutional character. They are standard; almost everyone knows about them and rather generally has theories about them which are often remarkably candid.

> Of course I don't tell my neighbors I took the traveling job so that Jan and I would be out of each other's hair a good deal of the time. I tell them what I tried to tell you at first—that I didn't really want the

job; that I was pressured into it; that I thought it would be a temporary inconvenience to help my career along. Actually, it's not that at all. I asked for it. It's a decision that we made together to try to hide our ugly little secret from the kids and the neighbors and even to keep from reminding ourselves of it at every turn.

One way or another, work away from home is a common solution. There may be traveling assignments, or the man (or woman) may be required to live at some place so far from home that commuting is impractical.

Separate bedrooms are also a common avoidance. It is not simply that the main intention is to avoid sexual contact. Since they know that they do not share in any vital sense, they feel as if this token of private acknowledgment somehow "makes the relationship more honest." Sometimes these are intended only as temporary expedients prior to an open break, "until the children get older" or "until I get reassigned." Repeatedly we were told that these separate living arrangements had evolved into permanent arrangements.

No activity is an avoidance device per se. Whether it is or not depends upon its *purpose* in the larger context of the relationship. One man's traveling job may be an assignment unsuccessfully fought off. A woman's devotion to church-related activities may be the natural outcome of deep religious conviction. Even separate beds may be due to some personal idiosyncrasy. One needs to know another person and himself quite well and to have information not ordinarily made public, before he can be sure that some activity is in fact an avoidance device for the one who is using it.

In addition to various conscious avoidance devices like those mentioned above, more insidious, unconscious forms also appear. Rationalizations are worked out so that one's avoidance efforts appear to him in a favorable light. He tells himself and others that he takes up a hobby or assumes some time-consuming civic responsibility because he enjoys such activities or is doing them in the civic interest. This is quite plausible, and even in a literal sense may be true, but it is not necessarily the real reason for taking on the activity. "You can't openly say that you find your wife so vacuous that you joined a club to fill the void." In time the substitute satisfactions—"sublimations" psychiatrists tend to call them—do become satisfying, if one has chosen well.

But mostly these people *do* know what they are doing. Both men and women frequently acknowledge that in their vigorous pursuit of a hobby or in their overdevotion to a job or in their overzealous religiosity, they are "compensating"— and they use that word.

> You know good and damn well that I'd rather be home romancing Eloise than out here on this weekend (fishing party). But she's a cold potato—at least with me—and I tell myself that at least if I'm out here with you guys, four miles from shore and with a cooler of beer and some ham sandwiches, that I won't be casually dropping in on those inviting spots along Euclid Avenue. . . . By the time we get back Sunday morning, I'll be too pooped to do anything else but sleep it off, take the kids on a picnic, and then it will be Monday. . . . How many of the other guys do you suppose, who come here every weekend all summer to fish, would be

here if they had something to talk about and something to get excited about with a woman in one of those cozy cabins along the shore?

And their wives are sublimating and compensating too—and they know it. So do their confidants. A clergyman offered an informed, and disarmingly honest, observation:

> I'm embarrassed to say this, but I think you suspect it. If there were more solid relationships between the husbands and wives in my congregation, we'd have a hard time keeping this church organized as well as it is. If the men and women were mated the way they ought to be, if their lives were full and their hearts full of each other, they would want to be together—and all those evening committee meetings and groups would dwindle to nothing. Why, half of our lay leadership is available only because there are such vacuums in their personal lives that they need something just to take up the time. Because they try to be decent people, they gravitate to the church. They think they will be safe here. . . . They come here just to work out their desertions at home by these binges of altruism. . . . And yet I suppose they would be worse off letting off their energies on less wholesome activities. Anyway, thank God, it's not mine to choose. But "spiritual" matters today are quite involved. . . .

Husband and wife sometimes participate in avoidance devices together, particularly in sports, "outside activities" and activities with children.

> Bob and I have a full life. Every night it's some-
> thing—and every weekend. . . . We're just so busy, we
> haven't time to think of ourselves. . . . We get so ex-
> hausted, we just drop into bed (with a sigh). . . . it's
> better than the cold shower is supposed to be.

Perhaps this embodies much of the practical value which
there may be in this kind of "togetherness." If enough activities of a sufficiently preoccupying and exhausting nature can
be participated in, the effort may succeed in taking the focus
away from the emptiness between the man and woman which
has developed or has been there all the time. It may also
divert attention from potential sources of alternative sexual
pleasure or from more open conflict.

A comforting illusion is often created for the outsider by
the person who successfully uses the avoidance devices. There
is something reassuringly "wholesome" about the avoidance
devices: the people using them have gone beyond the nasty
little temptations. If a man is sexually clumsy and uninter-
ested, his wife "solves" her problem by taking up Girl Scout
work and bowling. This is judged to be more "mature" than
looking for a better lover. It seems much better "to substitute
civilized fulfillment for the primitive need."

The deception implicit in the avoidance devices sometimes
becomes stark when the subject achieves spectacular success
with them. A writer saw this happen to his lifelong friend:

> Helen thought that a solution to her loneliness
> would be to go back to school—to do graduate work in
> the same field in which she had been interested twenty
> years ago in college. Her moderate talents, reinforced

by her enthusiasm, her pent-up energy, and her competitiveness with her successful husband moved her along rapidly. She did not so much work as pour her soul and her every energy into her new endeavor. She progressed quickly from an apt student, to an outstanding student, to a prodigy. Soon she became an authority in a highly specialized field of creative music. Her own sense of accomplishment was reinforced by the sincere and enthusiastic acclaim of others. The fame which settled upon her house took attention away from the fact that a once intensely man-oriented and vibrant woman had successfully carried out a binge of escapism. (This was verified by the woman's own testimony.)

Self-appraisal is as varied as self-expression. In some instances the person becomes aware of his diversion and make-believe; in others the avoidance devices are quietly and lastingly satisfactory. So some spoke of "having it made" in this way, or of having evolved a "sensible compromise" or of having become "adjusted" or of having achieved "maturity." Others are more sophisticated about it, a few even cynical, and quite a few sensitive about "this hypocrisy of living a public lie."

Linking the avoidance devices and the Utilitarian Marriage as we have may lead to the unintended inference that the connection between the two is more unilateral than we have in fact found it to be. The several reinforcements for the Utilitarian Marriage are numerous and subtle. Some have been discussed earlier: widespread feelings of mismating, diffuse sexuality in the work world, the career centrality, numerous passive-congenial and devitalized relationships. Meanwhile, there are the standard monolithic expectations as to how men and women should live and there are the special needs for a stable home base. Where there are also personal concepts which devalue deeper emotional expression and sharing, the Utilitarian Marriage provides the fitting constellation for adult living, child rearing, and discharging of civic responsibility. For the most restive, those who do not take so quickly or so passively to apathetic relations between the sexes and yet who do not wish to strike out a second time on the marital venture, the avoidance devices provide the useful opiate. This may be accomplished either with or without clandestine embellishment. Either way, the logic of combining good taste, personal achievement, and minimum risk serves to channel marriage into the quite conventional Utilitarian Mode.

The overriding inference from our inquiry is that the Utilitarian Marriage is shaped for most Significant Americans by a series of related, often unconscious, yet impelling choices. Once one sets his personal sights primarily on goals which lie outside the pair, once he thus devalues the private sphere in deference to some other, he commits himself, whether he realizes it or not, to an almost inexorable sequence of actions which culminate sooner or later in a full-fledged Utilitarian Marriage. For the passive-congenials it all comes quite undramatically and naturally; for the devitalized it seems about the only sensible way "at this time of life;" and for the conflict-habituated it serves about as well as any conceivable arrangement to contain the contest. Once set up, the valences are mutually reinforcing and the tide is therefore very hard to reverse. Chiefly, they do not want to reverse it; they are content with the current order of things, whether or not in other compartments of their minds they might like it otherwise.

Chapter 7

INTRINSIC MARRIAGE

ON the other side of the divide from the Utilitarian Marriages are the Intrinsic Marriages. To the people content with the Utilitarian Marriage, male-female relationships are tertiary to other matters of importance, clearly secondary to other things which must or should, they judge, come first. To those who want or need vital or total relationships (as described in Chapter 3), the relationship of a man and woman has top priority among the several considerations which make up a total life. These people, of course, also have careers, also must be concerned with public opinion, have obligations to children and the community; but typically they carry out these obligations and enjoy these privileges, while keeping them somehow subordinate.

A career woman married to an eminently successful man, each for the second time, characterized the basic contrast among marriages by an unconventional analogy.

Well, we've got a marriage-type marriage. Do you know what I mean? So many people—and me in my first marriage—just sort of touch on the edges of existence—don't *really* marry. It's funny, but my cookbook distinguishes between marinating and marrying of flavors. You know—the marinated flavors retain their identity—just mix a little—or the one predominates strongly over the other. But the married ones blend into something really new and the separate identities are lost. Well, a lot of people that I know aren't married at all—just marinated!

In the Intrinsic Marriage if there is conflict between obligations, the private and personal desires and needs of the pair come first. A high public official in an appointive position made the choice. He said:

I'll admit I'd rather have run for elective office. But my wife isn't comfortable with all the campaign dishonesty. . . . And a full life together is more important to me than being Senator. It's no sacrifice really. I just don't want to jeopardize or weaken the major satisfaction of my life for a minor one, even if it is important too. What would it profit me to try for a Senate seat and make it, if afterwards I found that our close and deeply sustaining life had been damaged in the process? How can *any* success be worth that?

Just as many in the Utilitarian Marriage have not exactly planned it to come out that way, or ever made a clear-cut, conscious decision to live their lives within such a structure, so also have those in the Intrinsic Marriage often evolved their present marital specifications quite unconsciously over the years.

A tall, lean, fifty-two-year-old scientist tried to recall the process by which he arrived at the philosophy by which he lives:

> From the time I was a child I never thought of it any other way. The first and central thing even in my adolescent fantasies was a close couple. I don't know how I came to see it this way because my parents certainly weren't especially close and I can't recall any particular pair who have set the model for me. It seems to come from the inside. . . . As I told you, I've had more than one marriage but the common element each time is this complete merging of myself, what I want in the personality of my woman and what she wants and does. I haven't the slightest interest in doing anything that I can't share with her or that she can't participate in with me. . . .
>
> Now that doesn't mean that we haven't differences —sometimes sharp ones—or that I haven't inhibited some desires because she doesn't want to share them. All I mean is that I just don't have or want to have any separate existence that amounts to anything. I do my work as well as I can—but—and I'm a little ashamed when I realize it—it doesn't have the importance to me that people think it does. As far as I'm concerned the whole corporation can go to hell any time if it infringes unduly on her, and especially on *us*, and the things that are precious to us. . . .

Some have moved deliberately, consciously, sometimes even ruthlessly toward Intrinsic Marriage. They have had another kind and found it unsuited to them. They use phrases like

"I just faced up to..." or "I sat down and took stock" or "I took a second look" and then made some major life re-orderings. There has been real tragedy in the backgrounds of some of the people now in these vibrant pairdoms. Just as there are people in the Utilitarian Marriages who say that they have "escaped from a stultifying relationship" with a former mate who had tried to hold them too close, so there are people in the Intrinsic Marriage who say that they have "graduated from the deadly prose" of some passive-congenial past.

Some of the characteristics of the vital pairs can be antic-ipated from this brief sketch. Obviously they do not feel mis-allied, although there is often a candid recognition that a spouse has some characteristics which the mate wishes were different. Despite the closeness with which they merge their lives and their identities, they are, nonetheless, able to recog-nize and accept acknowledged dislikes and disagreements. They also live under the impact of the intrusions which press upon people in this class, yet they are able to form and main-tain an intermeshing of personalities across the sexual line. For them "the miracle of mating" has become a preoccupa-tion, and the satisfactions from the marriage are intrinsic.

While there are exceptions, sex is usually important for these men and women. The words they use in talking about it are diagnostic. "It's not only important; it's *fun*." "It seems to be getting *better* all the time (at fifty-five)." "Sometimes I think my greatest satisfaction is in being so close to hers."

Sex for them is not something to be performed as a Satur-day night ritual. It pervades the whole life. At fifty-five a grandmother spoke poetically about it:

You can't draw the line between being in bed together and just being alive together. You touch tenderly when you pass; you wait for the intimate touch in the morning. Even the scents you make in bed together are cherished.

Some said they hid the importance of this part of their lives from others. From the perspectives of a passive-congenial world, a sexual emphasis at fifty-five *is* ridiculous. The intrinsically married sense this; they have heard the negative admonitions about acting one's age, keeping one's mind on other things, and all the rest.

Not only does sex tend to be solid pleasure for them, it's pleasure at *home*. With rare exceptions which we shall note later, most of them are not only monogamous but fiercely so. Probably this strong and satisfying monogamous accent is due to the tendency for these people to see the private side of life as a unity—sharply in contrast to those who chop it up into "phases" or "areas" or "sides." This holistic conception is described by the wife of a nationally known minister:

> I don't quite understand these references to the sex side of life. It *is* life. My husband and I are first of all a man and a woman—sexual creatures all through. That's where we get our real and central life satisfactions. If that's not right, nothing is.

The people in the Intrinsic Marriage are remarkably free of the well-known sexual disabilities. Frigidity is rare, as is impotency. Menopausal and menstrual disorders get scarcely any mention. These people are rarely preoccupied with their children's sexual problems or education. Their sexual joking is strikingly free of the familiar "sick" themes—perversions, homosexuality, impotency predicaments, senile and pre-pubertal difficulties.

And they have a lot of enjoyment besides sexual fun. Yet in their recreational activities nothing seems unique about them; they do the same things as the less vital pairs. All have access to the same catalog of fun and frolic provided by the modern affluent community. The main observable difference between those in the Intrinsic Marriages as a whole and those in the Utilitarian Marriages is that often the activities of the intrinsically married are much less standardized, less conventional, less formal. Some are clearly aware of this. One exurban wife confessed:

> Some of our friends think we're a little crazy living way out here in the sticks, spending so much time commuting and having the expense of maintaining our own private road, but we just like our little hermitage here—and so do the kids. Practically everything we do in one way or another applies to the maintenance of this little corner of the nineteenth century in which we live our lives.

Yet it is not the unconventionality of the activity which sets them apart; it is more the evident vitality, the close sharing, the joy of it all. One couple's do-it-yourself cabin in the mountains is for them an avoidance device; the other's across the creek is the product of total, vibrant sharing. "You can't tell the difference from the road."

People with Intrinsic Marriages often aren't very cooperative with the "community leadership." They are harder to

involve in civic and even in religious activities. It is not that
they do not see the worth of such things or that they do not
accept responsibilities on occasion. They simply scrutinize
the alternatives closely. When they "give up an evening" for
a civic function, they are much more likely to question
whether this enterprise is *really* important. Others think them
"a little irresponsible" because they ask such questions and
sometimes decline the invitation for no visibly good reason.

Another characteristic is that the wives go along, whether
it's a brief business trip in the evening or a month in Europe.
They don't go along to keep the husbands in line or merely
to help them keep up the proper public relations front. It
just does not occur to either of them that he would take the
trip alone, unless there were some urgent reason, like her
advanced pregnancy, or a sick child.

Such people seem strange, even incomprehensible, when
judged by the criteria of the Utilitarian Marriage. Those in
Utilitarian Marriages often voiced disbelief when Intrinsic
Marriages were discussed: "There are *no* people like that—not
after thirty surely." Or they're "oddballs" and "pretenders."
Yet it was sometimes also admitted obliquely that perhaps
something had been overlooked, that "they *must* have *something.*" Disapproval was voiced too. Some hoped that "these
immature people" might yet be brought into line somehow.

A man trained in psychology was confident that they would
be:

> Sooner or, later you've just got to act your age.
> People who stay to themselves so much must have
> some psychological problems—if they don't, they'll
> soon develop them.

It is also charged that in such marriages there is too much attachment to the spouse. Another psychologist vigorously asserted:

> Any man or woman who has to live *that close* is simply *sick*. He must need a mate as a crutch! He's too dependent! There's just something unhealthy about it.

A physician suggested to a wife that she take an extended vacation. When she explained that she would prefer some alternative because she and her husband were very close and his position prevented his accompanying her, the doctor countered with evident concern:

> In all these years, Mrs. Frank, that's the first neurotic symptom I've noticed in you.

Some complained to us that people in Intrinsic Marriages seem to neglect their children. They did not mean, of course, obvious neglect of the child's physical or educational needs. They meant that the parents are often so involved in each other that they are not sufficiently attentive to the concerns of their children. What seems at issue, however, are different philosophies of parental responsibility and child development. Some in the Intrinsic Marriages take a dim view of the way parents in the Utilitarian Marriages use their children as avoidance devices; they regard such preoccupation as more harmful than beneficial to the children. "Why, no son can absorb all the displaced love that a woman showers on him just because she's rejected by her eunuch husband," said one woman—who went on to say that she was compassionate, however, because she too had once had such a husband.

Some of the parents in Intrinsic Marriages are said to set a bad example for their children. They appear to be "too affectionate and much too frank about the intimate side of life. You'd think that life was one great big bedroom." They give this impression because they do not, as a rule, consider it appropriate to suppress or to conceal feelings which others either do not have or hide if they do. There may, however, be a complicating factor for the child—if he grows up to need or want this kind of marital mode for himself, he may not find many candidates who are suitable. His fraternity brother with a more conventional set of expectations and needs may find it much easier to mate.

A form of pretense was reported by some in Intrinsic Marriages:

> You know, if I told my neighbors or my husband's work associates at any of our parties how I really feel about him, and these other things I've told you, and what we do together, they'd laugh us out of the group. Well—not all of them. I suspect there are one or two couples who are a lot like us, but I'm not sure, because they don't say much either.

Most of the intrinsically married, however, seem not to be much concerned with what they consider a distorted view of themselves.

We talked to a few people with Utilitarian Marriages who looked across the fence with more than a little envy. Reflectively, stroking his chin, a sales executive said:

> By god, they do have something though. You feel it when you're around them. You should see the hell he

raises around the office when he has to go home a little
late, and the way he fights a trip out of town if he has
to go alone. I wonder what it is.

Those who are intrinsically married experience both sun-
shine and shadow, but it forms a different pattern from that
of their less-vitally married friends and neighbors. To feel
deeply content with a mate—to feel deep, moving involvement with his physical and psychological presence—is a kind
of well-being which they find richly rewarding and sustaining. From this fountainhead flow positive influences for physical and mental health, as well as for creativity. A substantial
professional literature in psychiatry confirms the testimony
of those in the Intrinsic Marriages that the vitality of their
kind of relationship radiates far beyond the elemental ecstasy
of the pairing.

Yet there are also shadows. In order to reach this point in
life, some of them have often had to pay the piper—sometimes
at an inflated price. They have had to turn their backs on
opportunities for other aggrandizements. Some say that it has
come very close to having to choose between the "invitation
to the dance" and the "invitation to the march." There are
men and women who told us that they had opportunities to
marry into families and fortunes but decided to forego them
in favor of a mating which would express what they considered to be their deeper selves.

A somewhat different calculation of price was evident for
those who made a first marriage which was perhaps motivated
by alien motives or by a misguided effort to be rational and
practical, or which grew out of some other misjudgment.
Later they discovered that they had a pressing need for an

entirely different kind of relationship and marriage mode. This kind of mid-life decision can be very costly for an Upper-Middle-Class man or woman, but some have paid the price.

Perhaps the darkest shadow is: "It's hell when it ends," whether by death or because "something went wrong." Despite the closeness, the empathy, and all of the other solidifying forces, Intrinsic Marriages have proved for some to be vulnerable. People who live in this way place enormous strains upon interpersonal relations, strains which are not present in the Utilitarian Marriage because the avoidance devices and the modest expectations about feeling and mutuality reinforce permanence "without cluttering up life with all that emotion." While some in the Intrinsic Marriages said they were clearly aware of this risk—or had already suffered the consequences of it—they are not for the most part preoccupied with it, except at moments of crisis. "You are so full of what you have that there's no time to be morbid. You live for the joys of each day together—not for the fears of a lonely tomorrow."

A jurist, fifty-one, summarized his discussion of the pros and cons in this way:

> This, then, is what it comes down to—you make an enormous investment in a woman and a marriage because you can't really do anything else—the dividends are enormous too . . . Why, I couldn't any more settle for the blue-chip conception of wife and marriage and family than I could rob a bank. Yet I know that my friends have deliberately and coolly done exactly that, and they seem to like it. I can't say even that I could

try it. I just can't have it any other way than this—and that's in spite of the fact that this is my second time around.

Men and women in Intrinsic Marriages experience conflict too. Some of these pairs actually have had more conflict than typically occurs for couples in Utilitarian Marriages. Partly it is simple mathematics. There are more numerous points of contact, hence more potential for conflict. Couples in Utilitarian Marriages often avoid conflict simply because so many important matters are considered private and not even exposed to the spouse. Also, the intrinsically married operate with a more exacting criterion for resolution of conflict. Because they have so much respect for each other and the relationship is so precious, the conflict has to be resolved in terms of the personal considerations as well as the practical issue.

The image of the Intrinsic Marriage which we have presented needs further clarification. The description has accented the totality of husband-wife sharing. Yet there are always aspects of life which cannot be shared, such as the details of career. But the emphasis on complete sharing is justified by the dramatic contrast to the pairs in the Utilitarian Marriage who touch at so few points. Similarly, we have stressed empathy and identification. Again, it is not black and white. We have seen numerous empathic aspects of spousal sharings in the Utilitarian Marriage. Such a wife may, for example, empathize with her husband's desire to keep the marriage on the periphery of importance, or he with her need to work out effective avoidance devices. But typically, empathy in the Intrinsic Marriage is not only multifaceted, it focuses upon the personal matters and so becomes an intense and pervasive quality of the interaction.

Despite the reinforcements which are built into the Intrinsic Marriage and which tend to make for continuity, there is no assurance that it will always remain so. Some of our interviewees related experiences with more than one Intrinsic Marriage. Each was unquestionably intrinsic at one period according to the criteria we have described, but when something came up which destroyed the closeness, the relationship quickly disintegrated. Under such circumstances, if there was no formal dissolution, the marriage continued but became a Utilitarian Marriage, since it had lost the essential qualities of Intrinsic Marriage. We also came across a few cases in which spouses in Utilitarian Marriages of long standing "discovered each other" and moved into an undeniably Intrinsic Marriage. Such sequences, however, were very rare.

There is nonetheless a basic uniform quality about the Intrinsic Marriage: the intensity of feelings about each other and the centrality of the spouse's welfare in each mate's scale of values. There was little doubt as to whether in each given case an Intrinsic Marriage existed. There are really no subtypes. The Utilitarian Marriage, on the other hand, encompasses a wide range of variations and degrees. Perhaps it is this diffuseness about the Utilitarian Marriage which accounts for its general acceptance by persons who wish to pursue widely variable life styles and yet maintain a marriage, home, and family. The requisites for an Intrinsic Marriage are much stricter. A personal merging so intimate and so encompassing does not come about by drift or default and cannot be sustained by listless attention to a mate. "You either have the whole splendid edifice or the damn thing tumbles down on you. There's just nothing halfway about this kind of life." Quite possibly this is one reason why they are in the minority.

Chapter 8

OTHER INVOLVEMENTS

THE Significant Americans associate with one another for long and important periods at the office, studio, or laboratory. They come from Utilitarian Marriages and from Intrinsic Marriages. Some are conscious of being mismated and are lonely in varying degree; some have an active sense of well-being where men and women are concerned. Some wish to put sexual matters as completely out of their minds as they can; others look upon the world of work as another hunting ground. Despite their intentions and often even promises to keep the personal and professional parts of life distinct, practically everyone acknowledges that it is difficult to pull off. Etiquette and morality aside, Eros asserts himself at the office.

Reference to the office is figurative. The Upper-Middle-Class man's office fans out on a large and diffuse stage. He works at airports and on trains, at cocktail parties and at the offices of his associates. He goes or is sent almost anywhere in the world for reasons of business or profession.

He works any time of the day or night—on any day of the week. It is difficult, if not impossible, for him to draw a sharp line between work and private life.

His work force is made up of both sexes and he often works very closely with women. This atmosphere of diffuse sexuality opens up opportunities and fosters relationships which many find it difficult to limit to the legitimate purpose. And others don't even remotely intend to. Thus, any realistic account of relationships of men and women in the Upper Middle Class should include not only marriage relationships but also those which are formed and carried on in the broader context.

The Significant American's wife meanwhile typically has little intimate knowledge of the subtle and important aspects of his work world. Even in those cases where he would like to share this world with his wife, he often finds it hard to bridge the chasm fostered by specialized language and the technical activities, but most of all by the strange values which pervade the enterprise. Some men have said that they feel they suffer the consequences of an inability to communicate adequately with their wives about career matters of enormous importance.

How do you go about explaining, without sounding like a sniveling coward, that you are *not* going to get that promotion, when your friend, who hasn't been there half as long gets his . . . How can you get her to understand what a snakepit this echelon of the corporation has become—and it won't get better for years. If she worked there, like my secretary, she'd know all about it almost before I do.

What knowledge of her husband's work world the wife has is usually fragmentary and stereotyped. It comes chiefly through secondary, symbolic evidences—income, promotions, changed titles, and miscellaneous feedback at the cocktail party or the protocol dinner.

Meanwhile the man's work associate very often is a woman, who is involved physically and emotionally in practically everything he does. She is a partner, a helpmate; her activities and efforts and attitudes must, if she is to be effective, dovetail neatly with his. A mutuality, if not identity, of purpose evolves. There is shared satisfaction when things go well, shared frustrations when they do not. Particularly where the relationship is enduring, it tends to take on a wifelike emotional and protective quality.

We use the phrase *office wife* for this widespread relationship with some hesitancy, since it conveys sexual meanings which the facts do not always justify. The office wife is usually a woman of superior intelligence and training who occupies a position of trust and responsibility as some important man's "Girl Friday." But it "says" much neater than it stays. A typical analysis came from a fifty-year-old executive secretary:

> You do get fond of him—almost in spite of yourself. At first you're a sort of chore girl, but as you learn the job better, you're entrusted with responsibility and get to know more and more about his worries, his humiliations, the ways his white hopes are dashed on the rocks of "policy." A decent human being cares, not in any impassioned way at first, but cares what happens to people she works with closely in this way. . . . If he looks a little worn, you bring him

a cup of coffee with just the right amount of cream and no sugar. . . . And you check his briefcase before the important conferences so that if he's forgotten an important paper in his harassment, you can spare him some embarrassment.

They say there is a gratifying sense of accomplishment in this, and that "if we do move into further involvement, particularly when there is reciprocation, it should be no surprise." The "further involvement" sometimes does and sometimes does not mean strictly sexual involvement. We made no attempt to take a census of either, although both admissions of sexual involvement and assurances to the contrary were frequently made.

There often is tacit, if not overt, reciprocation by the men. Men told us that they shared their private thoughts and fears and even hopes more with their office wives than they did with their wives at home. Repeatedly the phrase, "she understands better" came up. It seemed to us too, as we talked both with the wives and the office wives, that the latter do know more, and not merely more about the technical aspects of the enterprise. The claim of several office wives that "we know more about the deep, inner feelings of men than do their wives" was acknowledged as correct by many of the men. Why? Is it simply exposure, the many hours spent together, the mutual dependency? Or is there an acceleration of intimacy when the partner has continuing, important and common experience? Or is it the other side of the watershed of misalliance? Or the "unflattering polyeroticism of the species?"

One kind of answer came from a serious, forty-year-old scientist's assistant:

> We *do* have an advantage over the wives at home. If I help him draft a proposal that comes through with flying colors, I can really feel overjoyed at our mutual success, can feel that I have been a real part of it. But if the proposal falls through, I'm the one closest to his disappointment and I find deep comfort myself in my efforts to comfort him. . . . I haven't lost any status through his serious failures, as the wife at home often does. I have the advantage of understanding his feelings and knowing, after a time, better than anyone else how to take his mind off the slip-ups. Not just by patting him on the shoulder or smoothing his thinning locks, but by asking for his competent advice on the charts that are being worked out for the next proposal, or by reminding him of the tremendous reception his last speech had, and wondering aloud if that main theme shouldn't be worked into the next prospectus. The wife at home (and I'm one too) suffers by her distance from a very important part of her man's life. The woman at the office shares deep satisfactions whether the day goes well or not—she is needed and appreciated and she knows it.

And so the team is formed, solidified, and there is reported to be a deep personalization in working this way, for both.

Meanwhile the boss and the Girl Friday are both likely to be married—and not to each other. Kindnesses and considerations and carings of the sort which frequently develop are, by conventional definition, disloyalties to the spouse who has prior and superior rights. One must be secretive as a rule about the deeper meanings and sharings of the office partnership. This causes the relationship to become closer than it may intrinsically need to be, "because we share the secret knowledge that one or both of us must be protected from exposure at home."

Even when the husband is "understanding, broad-minded, emancipated, and all the rest," more than a little strain is created at home when the wife's work hours are not totally predictable, when in some occasional excited way she allows it to be known that the job is not so onerous after all, and when she shows defensiveness if some ungenerous observation is made about her employer. Such are the telltale marks of the office wife; "and even if they seem to tell things that are not true, the real-wife side of the total woman often knows when the office side has been exposed."

It is not always the case, however, that the office wife or her male counterpart is forced to play peek-a-boo with the spouse at home. Occasionally we found that this mode is understood and accepted. One wife, formerly a career woman herself, who is generally liberal in her views and self-consciously philosophical about serious matters, characterized the situation as:

> ... not only inevitable but an altogether sensible way in which to work out a life in this crazy, fragmentized world. ... What if she *is* a little more meaningful to him than interacting with a business machine? ... In another time it would have been some other arrangement.

In addition to the close relationships in the office there are the various opportunities which present themselves when a Significant American travels. Much of the time he is "entertained" on his trips or does some semiofficial entertaining himself. Variations cover a wide range, from activities appropriate for the local Sunday School picnic to a binge of wining and dining and call girls suggestive of the Roman holiday.

In the course of our conversations we came across several instances of "total entertainment." For example, one of the top men in a branch office of one of America's largest corporations keeps a small locked box in his office containing a card file of the important men who come to town with some regularity. Only he and his private secretary have access to the box. This file contains information on whether and what each man drinks and whether a girl is to be made available during his stay on company business. Many of our informants said that it is simply taken for granted that entertaining will include the privileges of bed as well as board, and both in some form suitable to the status of the guest. This is, as a public relations man put it, merely:

> ... the time-honored tradition of proper respect for the traveler away from home. If the corporation provides a fifty-dollar-a-night call girl (by another name of course) instead of the host's wife for the night, as among the Eskimo, the difference is trivial.

When the entertainment is not provided by the host, or when one is en route or has an evening to himself, invitations "to play a little" are said to be hard to avoid.

Wherever you go—to the cocktail lounge for a nightcap, to the theatre or concert, or just drop off in the lobby to scan a paper—there are other unattached people, you strike up a conversation, and bingo!

Sometimes these friendships are brief; they may or may not have an open sexual element, but the opportunities are there and the rationalizations to capitalize on them come easily. Over and over, from both men and women, we heard the same explanation. As one woman said:

After all, we're a broad-minded group of people, both the guys and the gals, and not stuffy about the old-fashioned notions. And besides, a fellow or a girl needs to have some fun once in a while, to let off steam and to raise a little hell.

The whole routine reminds some of them of earlier days when they were "civilian servicemen" (and women). Said a writer:

About the only difference is that today's "girls" (always a "nice girl" who is somebody's best friend) are the camp girls a little better put up and a little more expensive. Even if you don't care too much for that kind of a night, it's practically taken for granted. If someone else supplies the girls and the liquor and the hotel room—it's sort of a package deal. So why not?

These practices have passed the stage of being naughty oddities which only a few people know about. They are somewhat standardized, understood, almost institutional. Everyone in this group knows what they are and uses a consistent terminology for them, like the "pickup" which is described in many subtypes. Even those who profess to take no part personally are mostly not condemnatory or only mildly so.

Actual participation in these opportunities, of course, varies. Some men and women "have no part of it," either because they are "well taken care of at home" or because they profess "moral standards which do not condone such behavior under *any* circumstances." Others participate freely, but they do so on the fringes of their lives. A consulting engineer who rose rapidly to an executive vice-presidency, who called himself a "family man with a nice place in the country," described the practice of "living a little off the land":

> So you pick up a cute piece once in a while at an office party or when you're on the coast. She knows what she's doing and she likes it too. So what? I'm not at home, so I can't do the old girl any good anyway. . . . No, there's no continuity. Hell, I don't even know their names if I should want to look them up again.

Sometimes, however, there *is* continuity, especially where the object of sexual attraction is more continually available.

> Sure, I sleep off and on with Ross' secretary. It's not really an affair. Neither of us is exclusive about it. We just like each other that way. . . . Every once in a while we look at each other and sort of know it's about that time again. . . .

Other men and women have moved clearly beyond the mere business-related opportunities for expressing free-floating sexuality. Married or not, they acknowledge that they "live and date like single people."

For the married middle-aged of either sex, the date may lead to sex thrill or to an intellectual companionship at a lecture on nuclear physics. It may be cast in a romantic atmosphere, or it may simply be a somewhat longer than necessary ride home from some essential activity "like choir practice or having to work late at the office." The erotic element, the amount of secrecy, the amount of love involvement—all these and everything else they told us about the pairing is essentially parallel to the customary behavior of single people.

One of these married women is now in her late forties. Her husband is a prominent professional with a national reputation, highly respected in the metropolis where he works. They have two children—successful in school and immensely talented.

When I tell you that I feel quite happy, I don't mean that I'm happy just with my marriage—or any other one I can imagine having. My happiness is due to my wit and luck in working out a good life. . . .

First of all, I escape home through a job. It pays pretty well but, don't tell my boss, I'd work for nothing—just to have something interesting and challenging to do and to be around interesting people—chiefly, I suppose, men. . . . Then too, my husband and I live very independent lives—work and play—and you might as well know—sex too. When I tell you this, don't get

the idea that we sleep around promiscuously whenever a chance comes along. . . . We just live more or
less like single people—when something interesting
comes along, for either of us, we pursue it. There
may be satisfactions, mediocrity, or even disappointment at the end of the rainbow. But it's usually a nice
trip. . . . And this doesn't mean we have separate rooms
at home—or even beds. Far from it! Probably half of
the time—you see what I mean—it's us together. And
the rest of the time we're wherever luck takes us. . . .
It's all kinds—one-night thrills, affairs that have lasted
a year or two, a couple (of the affairs) have drifted
apart and then been reactivated, so to speak. . . . Yes,
I'd say my husband and I love each other—we just
don't own each other.

It's hard to say how we got into this pattern. . . .
One outgrows adolescence slowly and the one-and-
only-and-forever routine is sort of for kids, don't you
think? . . .

Gosh no, we're not unique. We know dozens of
couples like us. The details are different—sometimes
only one of the couple wants freedom—sometimes
they're not as open about it as we are. Sometimes they
seem to feel less sure of themselves than we do—but it
amounts to the same thing. . . . I'd say that this (pattern) may be present from the very start of a marriage
—a straight continuation of the single stage. Or it may
start later. . . . I suppose it could end, but I don't know
anyone who has given it up. Of course, none of our
friends are really *old* yet.

A single woman, forty-seven, a former university professor, is now employed in a high-ranking governmental position. She explains the role from the viewpoint of the unmarried woman. She has never married, but says:

> I prefer to date married men because they have a more natural attitude toward sex—single men are so self-conscious about it. . . . The best men *are* married but they also are quite available.

She has tried continued relationships with the same man

> . . . but it tends to get dull, or else gets too serious. I have a very married kind of attitude toward sex in relation to the rest of life—I want neither too much nor too little emphasis on it. I want it only in a larger relationship and in perspective. . . . I wear a diaphragm on every date. I don't always need it; and I insist that the rewards of the date do not depend on a sexual climax. . . . No, there's no problem around here in finding as good a milieu as married people have. No one cares any more, if you don't go out of your way to offend—well, like arriving without luggage, or being overdressed, oh, you know. . . .
>
> Yes, I'd say the pattern is common in Washington and other places in the East where I spend most of my time. . . .

She spends several weekends a year with men at homes of friends, some married and some not, who know about the arrangements, even though many of them do not practice such. She does not drink. She has had two pregnancies: "No regrets—except that I wasn't too bright at first and got pregnant when I didn't need to."

She averages two dates per week, with "about, oh, I'd say, every other weekend spent somewhere as a pair."

A man in his early fifties, holding a distinguished position in the communications industry, makes his point more philosophically:

> Marriage is simply an institutional arrangement for the immature—for the people who can't stand the strain of regulating their lives themselves—who need laws and public opinion and the Church to tell them what to do and what not to do. So, I'm all for marriage for the country and for most of the people. But not for me.... To do my best work, I need to be unencumbered—and even with the most ideal marriage I've ever seen, there is a lot of simple encumbrance.... You're probably wondering about sex. Well, I'm no eunuch—just disgustingly average, by Kinsey's tables, for my age and educational level. Now, there's no problem of finding good—in fact, I'd say excellent—sex partners wherever I've ever been—and that's all over the world. Before long you learn how to look for it and then it comes to meet you....
>
> That doesn't mean that all my sex life is a binge sort of thing. I have two sort of steady girls I have known and slept with off and on for twenty years—one is married; the other one isn't. I see them about as often as some of the career military men and State Department attachés see their wives.
>
> I have one son—eighteen now—a freshman at ———

(an Ivy League college). He was brought up by his mother and I see them both a great deal—only socially the past two or three years. Neither of us wanted to marry and, being Catholic, we just couldn't condone abortion, so she just decided to see it through. There was less social difficulty than we expected. . . .

Despite the well-known hazards purported to beset them, a rather high incidence of relatively enduring affairs was acknowledged by the men and women we spoke to. They vary widely from one another not only in details, but also with respect to the purpose they are said by the participants to fulfill. While sometimes they compensate for admittedly bad marriages which are held together for the sake of children or respectability or religion, at other times they involve people who say their marriages are fundamentally good. There seems to be a growing tolerance of the idea that some men and women need or want enduring sexual as well as platonic relationships with more than one person concurrently. Many who tolerate, or even approve, this kind of relationship admit that they wish the facts were otherwise, but "given human nature as it is and the world as it is, it just cannot be any other way."

Condonement of such relationships seems to come from a variety of motives. Sometimes, as in the following account by a wife, it comes more from resignation and empathy than from clear commitment to the practice.

Well, I've been a party to an affair for almost ten years now. . . . No, I said I was a party, not that I *had* the affair. You see, it all started this way. About ten years ago I noticed that my husband and the woman next door discovered a compelling interest in trimming the roses and the hedge between our two houses. They had practically trimmed all the leaves off. She's a fine person and I guessed they would like to know each other better. I knew they both liked bowling and I suggested they go bowling together. Her husband was away so I baby-sat with her kids. Since then, on two nights a week my husband and this woman go bowling together. . . . They usually come home about two. We don't say much about it, although everything is perfectly clear to all four of us directly concerned. . . . The neighbors? Well, by now they largely ignore it—at least we're not ostracized at any of the neighborhood social affairs. They may gossip about it, but there's so much else to gossip about that I don't suppose we get more than our fair share. A few years ago one woman did mention it to me and I quietly assured her that I knew all about it. That closed the case.

I would say that I am in love with my husband and the woman next door is in love with hers. Also, of course, she and my husband are in love with each other. . . . I don't think this has had any effect on our sex life as far as I can see. Of course, it's hard to say how things would be if they were different, but right from the start, I must admit that I thought it would either improve or worsen our intimate relations but it didn't do either.

No, I have not had an affair myself, simply for the reason that no good prospect came along. I am willing, but not eager. I can wait, but I won't fight it if it should come. . . . There are many designs for living.

This one is ours. If it's not ideal, it's better than a lot
I've seen, and whose business is it anyway?

Sometimes the "other involvement" was explained as
demonstrably beneficial to both husband and wife. In one
case the private secretary of a high state official (appointed)
often travels with him and when at home serves as his hostess
on virtually all protocol occasions. Her charm and poise are
obviously appreciated by the man, and she herself enjoys the
role. Whether or not there is sexual involvement we do not
know, but the wife seemed untroubled by the possibility;
she gave us this explanation:

> Bill does half his work over dinner or cocktails—
> he just *has* to do a lot of entertaining. . . . I'm sure he'd
> rather use our home, but I just can't do it. We tried—
> and I'm just not the hostess type. I'm a wife and
> mother and that's all I want to be. Bill's different
> when he's home with me and the children—he's re-
> laxed and fun. But when we entertained here at home,
> he was like a different person—all charged up, critical
> of me—I was always scared to death I'd do the wrong
> thing. I would get sick for days before an important
> dinner. . . . I'd get in such a state of nerves I didn't
> even recognize myself. I just can't try to be something
> I'm not. . . .
>
> I don't really understand Jane (the secretary)—but
> in a way I admire her—and Bill certainly needs her.
> I don't see how she can be so efficient—and she always
> looks right and says the right thing, never forgets
> names or faces—and everyone likes her. That's impor-
> tant. . . .

Bill's practically taken over one of the private dining rooms at the ———— Hotel for business and I can't tell you what a relief that is to me. . . . When he's home now we can just be a family—and I know he loves me and the children. He's a good man—and I'm a very happy woman. (They live in the country in a rambling nineteenth-century house so that she can "indulge in the good old-fashioned homemaking arts." She gardens, bakes, and sews, and cheerfully supervises their six children.)

In still other instances, the affairs are almost quasi marriages. A financier, who called himself "a fifteen-year veteran of a love affair" was one of several who do not link love and marriage in the conventional manner.

Frankly, I'm through with marriage. I've had it! Aside from the practical conveniences it brings, I can't see any advantages at all. We don't plan children at our age; we love and trust each other, and when we're together we both know it's because it's what we want more than anything else. When I go to her I do so knowing that this is what I want—it's not out of a sense of duty or convenience or because it's what everyone expects of me. The only thing that holds us together is our love for each other and that's the way it ought to be for a man and woman. In marriage everything goes stale. That hasn't happened to us in all these years. Why should we marry? It's more risk than it's worth.

Where the arrangement is more clearly a compromise, the man and woman in such a pair sometimes see it differently.

The circumstances, of course, may be more difficult for one than for the other. We have heard a great deal of impassioned resentment concerning the hard compromise.

> We live constantly in a state of suspension. I never doubt that he loves me, but sometimes it just doesn't make sense that he's still married to someone else. I know in his profession it's risky to have a divorce on your record, but there are risks this way too. What if people would find out about us? What would happen to his career then? It's such a strain to be covering up all the time—worrying about being seen where we shouldn't be, worrying about an apartment being "bugged," waiting for something to hit the newspapers. I don't know if I have the courage to go on like this indefinitely. We have so few times when we can both get away, when we can find an atmosphere of freedom. They're the times that sustain me. But must it *always* be this way? I feel as if we're living with something tragic hanging over our heads. And I can see no hope for any change. Do other people live out their loves this way?

In other instances habituation to conditions at first considered to be compromise brought an awareness that "one fits the role better than he at first thought."

> At first we talked a lot about getting married when we could both get free. But you know, I don't think it would really work. We're both such forceful people, I'm not sure we could stand being together all the time. When we meet now it's violent and passionate

and wonderful—and when we part, it's with a deep tearing at our insides. But we've gotten used to this—and when we're apart, we're both more productive than we've ever been before. Her latest shows have been her greatest successes and I've never had things more in hand. Knowing and loving her is the biggest thing in my life. She has sharpened my sensibilities, my creativity—I think I would collapse without her. We've had to work out an elaborate intrigue, but our life is full of crescendos—we do more real living in the hours we spend together than most people do in a lifetime. But maybe the living would be too rich for a steady diet. We both have commitments to other lives and maybe it's best that we do.

Another concluded casually:

It's like anything else in life. You try to balance out pluses and minuses and come up with something which is the best you can have under the circumstances. Nothing's ideal. But, all things considered, this is a pretty darn good arrangement for two people in love.

It is difficult, we found, to draw a line between enduring affairs such as these and arrangements which border so close on marriage that to call them "affairs" is to use a misnomer. Except for the legalities, the relationship is like that in marriage—the man (already legally married to someone else) assumes financial responsibility, spends as much time as he can with his "real wife," feels in love, and is identified as "father" by the children of this mating. The first marriage is the only legal one, of course, and that wife the recognized "status" wife in the formal community. The younger of the two relationships, although not necessarily involving a younger woman, must necessarily exist *sub rosa,* which is apparently not impossible to do in New York City or Chicago or San Francisco—and even in smaller places, we found.

These persons offered varied reasons for their conduct:

> Now you tell me, what is a man supposed to do when his Church tells him he can't divorce and re-marry, even though he and his so-called wife haven't really been man and wife for eleven years. We have nothing in common, not even spunk enough to fight, and both want nothing more than to be free of each other. I'm not taking that dictate like a slob—I've done something about it. . . . Sure, I'd *rather* have it clean and neat and honorable—especially for Helen. It's harder for her and for Chris too. Could be real bad some day. But Helen and I were in love and that love wasn't the kind of thing you get in motels and Carib-bean cruises—it was whole love and that means a place called home and a kid—to see yourself and her in an-other human life. It's worth taking the risks for—and God, I know they're big risks.

A similar situation occurred in several cases in which the wife refused to give a divorce. It should not be assumed that spite or other negative sentiments necessarily underlie such refusals. Sometimes we found that the considerations involved saving public face or protecting a family name or fortune. A case in point involves a physician who has built a suc-cessful and highly lucrative partnership in a private clinic with a small group of other doctors. Almost all of his wealth is tied up in the clinic—real estate, equipment, and so on—and in order to make a reasonable financial settlement with his estranged wife, he says it would be necessary to dissolve the clinic partnership. This would be embarrassing professionally, he fears, as well as financially.

So he and his wife have worked out a private agreement under the terms of which he maintains his home as before and spends some time there, and also maintains another home in a nearby city with his "real wife" and their two children with whom he spends considerable time, but not so openly as with the "status family." "In one way it's a hell of a life and in another, I feel so lucky that I'm not inclined to complain much." Both his wife and his "wife" confirmed the accuracy of the facts he gave us.

In other instances the motivations for refusing divorce are not strictly emotional ones. A few wives said that they even cooperate with their husband's maintenance of coexistent "marriages" because they recognize the legitimacy of the second relationship and yet do not wish to terminate their present marriages, which they still find somewhat satisfactory. It is not quite resignation—there is sometimes clear empathy for the second relationship, even though the wife nevertheless intends to retain her nominal marital status. One wife, estranged from her husband for almost ten years, prefers to maintain the form of the marriage, even though she gets no intrinsic benefits:

Of course I can see that they have the same right to happiness that anyone else does. I'd even go so far as to say that they have the *moral* right to it. . . . But why should *I* tear up *my* life—live as a divorcee, run the risk of financial problems later on when I'm older. . . . So, we worked it out like this. I'm sure he'd rather be free, and she too, and I feel for them. But I'm not sacrificial enough to go the whole way. . . . It's worked pretty well now for eight years.

They go on with these arrangements as the best they can work out for the psychological realities at hand, although they are quite aware that such patterns are not condoned by most people, even in their own somewhat practical and liberal class.

We discussed these relationships with an attorney in order to secure information relative to their legal status. He said that he had several clients who have evolved patterns of this type. He also confirmed our findings that the second "marriage" did not originate necessarily because of any manifest failure of the first marriage or necessarily from a refusal of the first spouse to agree to a divorce. The principals involved simply recognize "either that certain personalities cannot be encompassed in any one relationship or that compelling relationships between adults can arise after marriage as well as before." They honor the latter as they did the former ones as "being morally valid." As a rule, the first wife maintains the fiction publicly that she does not know about the second "marriage." Since she is likely to be in Russell Lynes' sense an "upper bohemian" rather than a true one, she finds it necessary to do so in order to pay homage to the public sanction system.

This is all not as unrewarding for the first wife, some said, as it might at first seem. She finds that freeing her husband from the restrictions of monogamy frees her too, and she may express her freedom in playing the role as if single, or in an affair of her own. Or she may do neither of these; she may simply continue to participate in a less than one hundred per cent relationship with her husband. Said one wife: "Having half of my husband is worth more to me than having one hundred per cent of any other man I have ever known." This was said uncomplainingly and without pretense that she would not prefer it otherwise. It was simply an acknowledgment of the status quo and a candid recognition that "life cannot always be fashioned from the maxims of the schoolgirl's copybook."

A clergyman in a large, predominantly Upper-Middle-Class congregation told us that he was aware of numerous such arrangements and had observed that

> . . . these always seem to be extremely vital and energetic people—people who have the capacity and the desire to live unusually fully. They seem to want to live two lifetimes in one life span.

And it does seem as if a few of them are able to achieve such an ambition with more vigor than other people can muster for one mating.

All is not rosy for the people with these *de facto* "marriages." Sometimes the problems and dilemmas are practical —insufficient money, how to divide one's leisure time, what to tell the children and when, and since the man is usually an important one, what to do if there is public exposure. They told us that they have discovered long since that one must stand ready to pay if one chooses to dine. Sometimes they "may misjudge the size of the check and may have to wash the dishes for a long time to pay off the bill." But typically this doesn't happen. They seem to move through life about as inconspicuously as anyone else—whether more totally fulfilled or not, one cannot objectively say.

The moralistic interpretation of all this would seem to some that these men and women are irresponsible and "sex mad" and that we have here presented an outline of their sordid sins. What such an interpretation misses may be the nub of the matter however. As we have pointed out previously, there is a pervasive loneliness for many of these people where man-and-woman matters are concerned. There is often a deep and serious lack of communication between many married pairs. This inability to share undermines the monogamous commitment. Couples may, and typically do, share various superficials, but these are not enough to dissipate the overwhelming awareness for so many that their spouses are "like different breeds." The strictly sexual stresses are there too, but mostly they are only outward symptoms of more encompassing loneliness, of desertion, or of felt need for a fuller participation than has yet been attained. Much research has documented the fact that men and women vary enormously in the amount and kind of sexual expression they need and desire. Often they are very unequally yoked in marriage in this respect, and yet do not wish—or one of them doesn't—to dissolve the marriage so that each may try again.

It should be clear, however, that these modes of adaptation are not necessarily or exclusively sexual with respect to the satisfactions which they are said to bring. The patterns, we were told repeatedly, are typically established to relieve more total stress. The enduring affairs and much of the dating too, have a low sexual component as measured by frequency or centrality of sex. While short on sex, they are said by the participants to be long on understanding and empathy. Yet there is no denying that the sexual valence is there. Typically, it is not there as sex per se; it is more an emergence of human totality. "After all, we are male and female," said one, "and I suppose sex *is* the ultimate means of communication between people who care."

This may all seem to be a scandalously amoral dismissal of a serious matter. How about higher motivations, good example, and responsible citizenship? To say nothing about proper respect for the proscriptions of the Deity. Is personal satisfaction all there is to it? Is a self-focused hedonism the appropriate end for human conduct? The Significant Americans whose relationships have provided the substance for this chapter find such "cosmic considerations" largely irrelevant and immaterial. The deviants are rarely, if ever, troubled by such matters. Obviously, they don't enjoy the acrimonious remarks about themselves, but they mostly shrug their shoulders and go on their way, convinced that they have the *right* to seek love and happiness in their own way. Said a doctor, "I have examined my conscience in the matter and I feel anything but guilty." While hardly a definitive discourse on morality, his remarks do reflect what these people think about their own situations. On the whole they are neither troubled nor self-consciously philosophical about what they are doing. They are simply making the best of the opportunities presented by a confused and contradictory societal context in order to satisfy their deeply human needs.

Chapter 9

AGAINST THE GRAIN

WE found several patent features of the private lives of
the Significant Americans which sharply contradict concepts
about men and women, sex and marriage, which are widely
accepted as accurate and reliable. Some of these findings not
only run against the grain of American culture but they also
run counter to much professional opinion too. A few are reassuring to those who hold traditional views—others are
threatening to the conservative conscience. But sustaining or
frightening, they press for exposure.

It is a commonplace that sexual themes pervade American
society. Popular literature and music express a frank preoccupation with sex, often in its rawest aspects. Madison Ave-
nue incessantly exploits vulnerability to sexual stimuli. It is
said to be almost impossible to isolate oneself or one's children from the pelvic ethos.

Yet this pervasive accent on sex seems not to have much
shaped the habits and tastes of the Significant Americans in

line with the ubiquitous image. Many remain clearly ascetic where sex is concerned. Others are simply *a*sexual. For still others, sex is overlaid with such strong hostility that an *anti*-sexual orientation is clear. In sum, we found substantial numbers of men and women who in their present circumstances couldn't care less about anything than they do about sex. Sometimes this sexual apathy is merely a continuation of lifelong habits and interests which the sexual thrustings of the mass media, commercial recreation, and the arts have not modified. In other instances, however, present interests and feelings are in clear contrast to earlier ones—but still against the alleged cultural grain. But whether now devitalized or never having been vital, the overriding fact seems to be that for the majority, by the middle years, sex has become almost nonexistent, something to be stifled, or a matter about which they are downright afraid and negative.

A closer look at particular cases helps illuminate the reasons for this widespread devaluation of sex. If, for example, a man has lived with a frigid woman for twenty years, a woman "who has managed to get a good ten-year total mileage out of premenopausal, menopausal, and postmenopausal tortures," his bitterness and sheer fatigue may understandably result in his disengagement from the whole activity. Yet, another man, coming out of the same configuration, quietly and unobtrusively seeks sexual vitality with another woman.

In another familiar configuration the man or woman remains sexually normal according, say, to Kinsey's tables, but in conversations about sex is negative and hostile. Often he does not spare himself, frankly asserting that he finds sex "a damned nuisance," but one which he yields to now and then "with a minimum of fanfare." Some, the women especially, outwardly express fear of sex in general and especially of the real or assumed sexuality of their unmarried sons and daughters. Some are so openly resentful about the impelling nature of sex in the lives of their children that they can no longer yield to the sexual feelings and opportunities which occasionally arise for them in their marriages.

Men, too, are well represented among the sexually disengaged. One of our interviewees, a nationally known psychiatrist, commented:

> By forty, a majority of American men in this social class are so emotionally crippled, confused, and generally neurotic about sex in their own lives that they are washed up.

He went on to explain that he did not mean that a majority were incapable of the sex act, impotent in a technical sense. Rather, he said, their attitudes and practices have become so overlaid with anxiety, hostility, and accumulated failures that there occurs a *de facto* impotency; they are unable to give or to receive gratification as they may have in their earlier years. In a variety of contexts many of our subjects gave us information which essentially sustained this psychiatrist's observation.

A few standard difficulties and aversions were reported frequently by the women. Sexual inadequacy is one. The currently great concern about the high incidence of orgasm inadequacy in women seems, however, to be only part of a much larger problem. Despite the free discussion of the subject there are women, otherwise quite knowledgeable, who are still vague as to what is meant by "sexual climax" or orgasm. These women appear to confuse generalized, diffuse sexual excitement with technical orgasm. What seems even more important to report is the large amount of expressed dissatisfaction with sex in general among women who implied that they did experience orgasm but still remain apathetic or negative toward sex.

Perhaps sexual satisfaction is so strongly influenced by the rest of their lives that physical-psychological capacity for orgasm is not really the nub of the matter. A very vigorous woman, a former college French teacher and mother of two high school children, expressed a common lament:

> How are you supposed to have decent sex with a man who sees nothing really good or fun about it? He performs—that's his word for it—the sex act in a routine, unimaginative way now and then—mostly when he's had too much to drink. Whenever he talks about sex, his resentment gets through more than anything else. . . . How can I let go and enjoy myself in an atmosphere like that? It's a wonder I haven't jumped the fence as many of my girl friends have. After a while you just get used to it—you shrivel up inside. . . .

A physician, fifty, athletic and vigorous, regretfully described a similar atmosphere:

> She doesn't really refuse me—just so casual and submissive and matter-of-fact—like it's part of the weekly toilet or the formal etiquette of marriage. She seems to enjoy certain moments—like it was in spite of herself. But there's no *joie*, you know, no evidence of anticipation, no pleasant talk afterwards. It's like cop-

ulating with a well-tuned, delicate machine. . . . Pretty
soon you don't give much of a damn about it yourself. . . . A lot of men I know say the same thing. Sometimes they blame themselves and sometimes their
wives. But there just doesn't seem to be much there
for a lot of us.

Sex is to others something like a practical joke on the
human race; not exactly a curse—just a ridiculous predicament. It provides some comforts for them now and then,
they say, but it is mostly like any other body function—it
needs attention from time to time and then some sort of
release follows. "That's about all there is to it." The ones
who bear the brunt of the joke are considered by these people to be the ones who take sex seriously—the fall guys who
expect it to be deeply satisfying and lastingly so, who try to
"build a Taj Mahal around every piece." These people, on
the other hand, think they have sex really mastered and never
make such a mistake—at least not after they have "grown up."

On the surface this devaluation of sex may seem inconsistent with what the subjects of the study told us about
their other involvements. Not so. First, their "other involvements" cover a wide variety of sexual—and sometimes not
sexual—relationships. There is no inconsistency between de-
valuing sexual fulfillment as a life goal and "shacking up now
and then" when in Paris, or after a wearing conference, or
when the wife is off to Hawaii. In fact, it can be cogently
argued, it seems to us, that the person who devalues sex may
be somewhat more likely to express himself in noncontinu-
ous, nondemanding, and possibly debasing "sexcapades." At

least he (or she) thus tacitly acknowledges that it's all sort of casual, an unimportant part of normal life.

This is not so for that minority with the enduring affairs or those who "tore up a former life at midstream for a warm bed and a soft body." And not so either for the intrinsically married who mated as whole people in the first place. But these, even when taken together, are clearly a minority, however romantic and occasionally poignant their portraits may seem.

The widespread devaluation of sex may all be a reaction, of course, against the symbolic sexual preoccupation of the larger society. Or it may be a consequence of middle age. Or, what is called sex drive is perhaps being channeled into careers or intellectual pursuits. The difficulty with these tempting summary interpretations, however, is that the sexually aggrandizing people, those who say they enjoy and value sex expression as an important life focus, also live in the same culture, are also middle aged, and are also successfully fulfilling their demanding career obligations.

Many among the Significant Americans profess considerable sophistication about psychological and psychiatric concepts, particularly as they relate to sexual and marital matters. Almost all of them have friends, acquaintances, or relatives who have "gone to the couch" or have been treated by professionals such as marriage counselors or clinical psychologists. And they have all read at least popular accounts of the presumed causes of mental-emotional disturbances and have frequently seen these themes developed in novels and plays.

As we compared our information about these people with some current psychiatric ideas, one inference was hard to escape: psychiatric clichés, particularly as used by laymen, are much too pat to square with the facts as they were given to us.

The presumed linkage of guilt and moral deviation is a case in point. Running through the popular, and to some extent the professional, conception of mental illness is the strong inference that people who violate the dictates of the monolithic code are the ones who suffer deleterious mental-emotional effects. Thus, for example, if a woman has had an abortion or has been promiscuous before marriage or has had an affair, there is a tacit assumption that such behavior is "bound to produce emotional trouble for her. She'll be guilty, get psychosomatic illness or worse—you'll see." And almost everyone knows of cases in which such linkages appear to be correct: so and so did err and she, or he, is now having serious emotional troubles, Q.E.D.

What many amateurs miss, and even some of the professionals, is that there has been no systematic count of, say, women who have had abortions, or been premaritally promiscuous, or been involved in one or more extramarital affairs, but who have not subsequently become emotionally disturbed, much less severely ill. Such self-directing people—our data suggest a clear majority of them—simply do not develop the overpowering negative emotional residues that they are supposed to, according to the simplitudes of textbooks on mental hygiene or on how to be happy though married. It seems pertinent to note that in this group of 437 eminent people, so many calmly acknowledged that they had in fact done, or are now doing, the things which are supposed to lead to psychological disaster; yet no such disaster has occurred. Quite the reverse—they remain healthy, creative people whose talents help to give direction to the collective human enterprise.

And yet the notion of a necessary connection persists, even among professionals. An occasional one recognized his "curious mind-set" on the matter:

> You know, when I was in med school, practically all the fellows in the fraternity slept around pretty freely with the girls in the sorority down the block. I'm not boasting, but I think it's factually true that nine out of ten of us were involved one time or another with nine out of ten of those girls. Several got pregnant; none of them got married in college, and all but a couple of them (who got pregnant) had abortions. Some went through hell for a while and so did we, but before long these things heal ... and you know, I've kept track of an extraordinary number of them over the years and they're doing remarkably well. Still, when I think about abortion, I always assume that if a woman has one, she's going to wind up on the couch. It's the same way with other things, say, sexual perversions, and homosexuality, and promiscuity among adults. I know from my own clinical experience that often they don't make a damn bit of difference, but I still have a mind-set. . . . I wonder if I've ever put ideas into my patients' heads and so contributed further to their disturbance. You know, suggested to them that they *ought* to be troubled ...

Some of our subjects acknowledged that they did feel guilty about one aspect or another of their past or present conduct. Some men, for example, felt guilty about their extramarital affairs and some women, about their abortions. However, most of them with such experiences expressed no guilt and said they would do exactly the same things if they had the same choice again. We found very little evidence of guilt about unchastity or adultery. Most of the regret we did find had to do only with the more peripheral considerations, as in the case of a woman who said she did not in the least regret her promiscuity but was ashamed of some of her choices of partners.

Regret should be distinguished from guilt. Our people often expressed regret that they made some choice or another, but they didn't usually feel guilty. They interpret their misjudgments or miscalculations as human frailties or bad luck, and if they feel regret about practical outcomes, it is not necessarily connected with moral guilt. There are, for example, recurrent cases in which married persons later regretted their affairs but only because they came to light and embarrassed them or their children. Or the woman who had an abortion and regretted it, but only because there were later health complications. Regret over practical consequences, then, is to be sharply distinguished from guilt— which amounts to a negative self-definition concerning the act itself, regardless of whether the act brought pleasure or pain, fulfillment or frustration.

Sublimation, too, can do with a second look. In recent years it has been intellectually fashionable to point out that sexual sublimation is exceedingly difficult to pull off and quite dangerous to mental health should one succeed. The people who provided the information for this study challenge both of these assumptions. Many of these career-dominated people have channeled almost the whole of their energies into success aspirations. For some it had been practically a necessity to do so in order to complete their education and carry the grueling responsibilities and work loads of their early years. Some now regret that they were as successful at sublimation as they were; now they would like to recapture the sexual vitality which they relegated to disuse, but they have become different people and it is impossible to go back. We are, of course, dealing here with a highly educated group of people, a selected group in the sense that they have demanding jobs which usually require a great deal of discipline. In other classes the frequency and success of sublimation may be very different. Nevertheless, a great many of these prominent people have been able to inhibit the sexual side of their nature without visibly jeopardizing their mental health or their spectacular career success.

Some, of course, seem to have paid for successful sublimations—depending on what one means by "paying a price." It is very difficult to weigh a distinguished scientific or diplomatic career built by endless hours of hard discipline against a presumably enriched personal sexual life which the subject might have had if he had lived more like an ordinary man. This raises questions of moral value which go beyond considerations of individual frustration or fulfillment. It can and has been argued that talented and highly placed people have a public responsibility to make whatever personal sacrifice may be entailed in order to carry out their obligations to society. At least some of the Significant Americans accept this logic and defend it as an altogether reasonable requirement.

Furthermore, what is often interpreted as sexual sublimation in the interests of career has in many cases not been sublimation at all. For some people there has always been low sexual energy or absence of sexual awakening, hence no pressing libidinal urge to be inhibited. It has been suggested in much serious professional writing that low sex capacity may be associated with outstanding academic and later occupational achievement in just this way. Whatever the cause and effect connection, it is in line with the self-description and self-analysis of a substantial minority of those whom we interviewed that the absence of a clear sexual valence in their lives is not the result of deliberate inhibition. "It's never been that important to me—much less a problem."

Another prevalent view held by many laymen and some professionals makes a dubious, or at least too categorical, linkage between deviant behavior and subsequent negative practical outcomes. Thus, the premaritally promiscuous woman, quite aside from moral issues, is typically said to have jeopardized her chances for marital happiness. The logic is widely diffused—she'll find it difficult to settle down to one man; she'll suffer a bad reputation; her past will turn up and embarrass her. Similarly, the woman with the extramarital affair is said to be destroying another woman's home, and possibly her own, and both she and the man will sooner or later suffer serious consequences; at the very least, the risk of exposure will seriously interfere with their happiness and security. Whether or not these linkages are true at other class levels, they have not typically been true for the people in this one. Not that it is impossible to find instances of such, but rather that we have found many more instances in which the disapproved conduct did not result in the predicted personal disaster and it is now judged by the subjects to have had positive benefits for which they are often deeply grateful. We talked with women whom abortions had protected from an undesirable marriage which they would otherwise have felt obligated to enter into. Some women, and some men, were grateful that they did not bring their sexual innocence to their marriages, and were instead able to use some worldly wisdom on sex to further their own and their spouse's gratification. And, it will be recalled, some of the extramarital involvements are judged by the participants to yield more benefits than difficulties.

Yet our data do not sustain a wholly casual view either. Some people among the 437 have, they said, experienced guilt, shame, and emotional discomfort in varying degree, as a result of their reflection upon their sexual deviations. But the extent of disturbance has been highly variable in apparent cause as well as intensity and much seems to depend on other qualities in the larger relationship. A moralistic husband, in whom a woman has confided some transgression, for example, may have a totally different reaction to her than would an accepting, permissive husband with the same information. The moralist quickly reasons that since the act is disapproved, he has a perfect right, even a responsibility, to be condemnatory toward her and that she is merely getting her just deserts for transgressing moral law. Yet a deterioration of the marriage would have been avoided by his tolerance quite as much as by her abstinence from the deviant behavior in the first place. As a matter of repeatedly reported fact, it is exactly such a condition which makes the linkage between deviancy and subsequent destructive consequences as equivocal as it has been in the lives of these people. Understanding, permissiveness, tolerance, and empathy have been, and currently are, the great healers; moralism, dogmatism, inability or unwillingness to understand have been, over and over again, seriously toxic agents.

There is widespread supposition that behavior emerges from forces within people, from their "personalities." In this view a person is inherently constituted so that certain kinds of behavior are almost predictable. People are thus characterized by such terms as intelligent, oversexed, excitable, stable, energetic, apathetic, moral, conservative or what not, and it is assumed that they behave as they do because they "are" this way. A prima-facie plausibility supports this; almost anyone can select illustrations to show that some person known to him reacts more or less predictably in certain ways. Hence the strong case for "personality" as an explanation of conduct.

This seems, from our observations of the Significant Americans at least, to be an insufficient and sometimes seriously deceptive explanation. The nature of *relationship* is also causative—and importantly so. To illustrate, possibly oversimply at first, let us take the case of the "mother-in-law." Consensus, supported by observation, has it that mothers-in-law are less tolerant, less affectionate, more critical, more interfering, and so on, than are mothers. Yet a mother-in-law must also be a mother. Her mother-in-law behavior and her mother behavior are observed, nonetheless, to be different, and even opposite. What, now, is her personality? Which of the two behavior sets is her real, or basic, or true personality? If the answer is, as it must be, "both," then her personality somehow embraces opposite habitual actions and presumably accompanying feelings. There is still the need, then, to explain why in one context she is typically and predictably kind and empathic, and in the other one cold and critical.

More to the point for our own inquiry is an instance which we came upon early in our investigations and for which we have since found numerous counterparts. One of our women interviewees had been married for fifteen years and had been involved for five of those years in an affair with a man with whom she was deeply in love. In the sexual relationship with her husband she had always been frigid; she had experienced only one or two orgasms in fifteen years of marriage. She insisted to her husband and to others, when she was called upon to discuss the matter, that sex was not important to adults and that things other than sex were—children, career, culture. Although she read widely, she avoided psychological literature, particularly if it involved sex. In the other relationship, she almost always experienced multiple orgasm and an extremely high frequency of sexual intercourse. She consequently became exceedingly interested in learning more through reading and conversation about the sexual side of life. Now, how is one to say whether her personality is positively or negatively oriented toward sex? Is she frigid or is she deeply sexual?

We have abundant evidence to demonstrate that the interplay of two people, and not merely the attributes each had beforehand, visibly resulted in the behavior which characterized any given relationship. Much more often than not, the same persons showed radically different behavior with different persons of the opposite sex, whether the relationships followed in sequence or occurred intermittently with one another. Personality, however much may be known about it, is not an adequate gauge to accurately anticipate or thoroughly understand people interacting totally in their personal dimensions. The Significant Americans themselves seem to have learned this as they explained over and over again "how different" they felt and acted in different relationships with the opposite sex. Acting on this principle (or faith) many of them, as we have seen, have turned away from relationships which brought forth negative attitudes and actions, formed new relationships, and went on to find a renaissance of comfort and well-being.

Five years after such a choice, a mother of four children defended her action in terms similar to those used by numerous others. (Although this woman had at one point turned to professional help, she is included in the study because she terminated her "therapy" after only two or three sessions.)

> I had become a psychological mess and I knew it— so did my husband, and so did my friends. The kids didn't miss it either. So I left him . . . It's a lot quicker, less costly, and less disorganizing than going to the couch. I know. I tried that too. All I got from it was a feeling of resignation and apathy, which I almost went for . . . But I couldn't really learn to live with the nothingness. . . . What I needed was the right man . . . Now everybody say's I'm so different—my health, my appearance, my outlook, my work—everything!

Another widespread supposition, particularly among people who have faith in the efficacy of religious institutions, holds that there is an important causal connection between religious participation and the kind of marriage and family life which people have. The simplitude, "Those who pray together, stay together," tersely expresses this view, although in fairness, not everyone takes it so literally. Many assume a less direct linkage, pointing out that "the ideals of love, respect for individuality, and religious ceremonies have a moderating influence on passion and hold up high personal goals" which are further reinforced by association with a community of similar believers.

Among the 437 there were Catholics, Protestants, and Jews and also those of no stated religious faith or identification whatsoever. An additional category, nominals, were people who once had been actively identified with a religious faith but had broken with or drifted from the church, usually in early adulthood. Comparing the people in these categories (See Table p. 8), we could find no clear differences with respect to any of the information which they offered about themselves, except for one. Among the active Catholics many said that they respected the Church's position on divorce and would not challenge it. Some Catholics, on the other hand, did challenge the position and got divorces by subterfuge (for example, annulment—after nine years!) or by open defiance. Also, distinctly antidivorce comments, as well as actual decisions not to divorce even though quite unhappy together, came from people with no religious commitments whatsoever. We heard some very austere moral codes from persons of no religious identification or who were adherents of faiths which are officially quite liberal. Within each of the five marriage types we found representatives from all major religious groups—and those who professed no faith. The church-identified were no different as a whole from the non-committed in any *actual* (as distinct from verbal) conduct which was described to us.

We do not mean to suggest, however, that religion is therefore without any influence in these matters, because in our conversations with some of these people it was clear that the beliefs and prohibitions of the various churches are taken seriously and efforts are made to translate them into concrete action. But to take a principle seriously is not the same as successfully ordering one's life in accord with it.

There is a caustic literature coming from the pens of high church leaders in all faiths, which decries the impunity with which many of the church-identified people violate the principles and practices of their faith. Our findings are clearly consistent with these critics', except, of course, that we have examined people in only one class and only in their male-female attitudes and actions. Membership, attendance, and even active service to the church are not highly correlated with actual moral and ethical commitment to the teachings of the churches.

Nowhere did we find this more clear than on the subject of sexual morality. These people typically offered judgments about what is and what is not acceptable which bore practically no relation to what their own churches had been teaching for centuries. It is commonly acknowledged, for example, that Upper-Class Catholics largely ignore the Church's advice on contraception, advice which is said to be taken much more seriously by the less educated. Even the clergymen with whom we talked seemed disinclined to make much of an issue of traditional moral strictures. Apparently, a kind of liberal humanism has come to be accepted by top level clergy —at least in private conversation—which is much like the liberal humanism we found so general among the rest of the Significant Americans. Insofar as they expressed views, what they had to say seemed more to concern practical matters and consequences than the inherent immorality of the acts.

A general confusion between instrumental judgments and morality per se is seen almost everywhere. One housewife had the distinction clear:

> You are told that you should not be adulterous because you might have an illegitimate child, your husband would divorce you if he found out, or you would feel forever guilty. But that logic is all wrong. If you follow it, then quite logically—if you employ reliable contraception, your husband grants permission, and you don't in fact feel guilty—there is no need to heed the dictum. But if adultery is wrong, categorically and unequivocally, then the consequences, whether tragic or nonexistent, are completely irrelevant.

There is throughout American society this clear tendency to put traditional moral issues into pragmatic terms, although, as this woman cogently pointed out, to do so is to set the stage for denial of the principle. Perhaps, then, the Significant Americans who tend, with exceptions to be sure, to follow the pragmatic tests alone do so with much convention on their side.

Morality in its collective dimension is, however, difficult to infer from conduct directly. First there is the broad cloak of concealment. Marriage itself, as we have seen, is often such a facade: men and women in enduring marriages often make a shambles of the noble sentiments presumably incorporated in their stable support of the marital institution. There is also the seemingly moral stance, but it comes from the absence of opportunity rather than from commitment to moral precept. For example, we were told over and over again by both men and women that they stood ready to participate in adulterous relationships (usually designated by euphemistic words like affairs, intimate friendships, and involvements) but had not as yet done so pending discovery of a suitable partner or of the right practical circumstances to consummate their intentions. Even if these people never find the right opportunity, the moral precept is already violated by the intention; they have served notice, if only to themselves, that they reject the moral code on this point. Similarly, the misallied, who say quite candidly that they would seek a divorce if they could get the sanction of the Church, or the consent of a reluctant spouse, or find adequate financial resources, are monogamous only by default—not by moral commitment. Given the opportunity, they stand ready to act in a way which the monolithic code disapproves. They often await such opportunities with eager, if not always hopeful, anticipation.

We are not, to be sure, concerning ourselves with the sticky question of what specific acts are or are not moral. Instead, attention is being called to the twin facts that in the ecclesiastical heritage and elsewhere, a set of established prescriptions for moral thoughts and deeds is firmly established; and at the same time a *de facto* set of widespread practices breaks at important points with almost all of these precepts. A prevailing interpretation comfortably assumes that since over ninety per cent of the adult population is married, and three out of four marriages remain unbroken, and that since publicly known and verified instances of infidelity are few, the moral order is therefore a true order; that people mostly accept it and live by it. Simple fact often makes a mockery of such assumption. Established and enduring marriages often perpetuate relationships between men and women, as we have seen, which are utterly immoral by the broader precepts of the very code which seems to be honored. Concealment and cynical manipulation in the interest of a useful public image are rampant. Absence of opportunity, rather than moral commitment is acknowledged as a further distortion of the extent of real adherence to the moral order. These and other unheralded facts converge to cast a long gray shadow of doubt over the sunny optimism of some of the Significant Americans.

In our discussions with the 437, no one point of view emerged which could accurately be called a typical woman's view or typical man's view; the same for overt conduct. The differences we found, many of them sharp, are differences *among* women and *among* men.

Strictly moral attitudes were reported as frequently by men as by women; promiscuous life patterns were reported roughly as often by women as by men. Empathy, or the lack of it, is also not the exclusive property of either sex. Compassionate, almost impassioned, concern for people caught in one or another predicament was often expressed by men, while women often voiced the most austere and unforgiving disapproval—this on any subject—abortion, divorce, childlessness, call girls, career women. Even though the worlds of men and women are still quite different in a number of obvious respects, apparently the modern pressures which shape diverse practices and varied attitudes affect the two sexes in ways which are so similar that the attitudes of men and women are not significantly different from one another.

Meanwhile, books are written, sermons delivered, clinics held, and magazine articles published on "the woman's view" of this or that, or how a Protestant family or Jewish or Catholic family is presumed to live, and even what the marital problems of college women will be. Possibly in another time or in some small pocket of the population, such categories may occasionally be predictive of actual attitudes and behavior, but not for the class investigated in this study and probably not for the bulk of American society either. In innumerable matters, there are of course, differences between men and women, between communicants of the several religious faiths, between people in various occupations; but insofar as the relations between the sexes is concerned, the actual beliefs, actions, and intentions of the Significant Americans do not importantly follow these categorical lines. Their relationship types, marriage forms, moral conceptions, past actions, values —just about everything they talked about—cut across the conventionally used lines of delineation almost randomly. Whatever usefulness the traditional categories may have, they manifestly tell us very little, if anything, about the relationships of men and women as we came to know them in this highest echelon of the American Upper Middle Class.

Chapter 10

OVERVIEW

IF we learned anything from our long and intimate conversations with these 437 Significant Americans, it is that no summary generalizations about the connections between success in public life and success in the private, marital sphere squares with the facts as they were given to us. These people differ among themselves sharply and often irreconcilably. They break over basic values pertaining to men and women, the most radical being the question of whether this dimension of life is its essence or only an auxiliary to some other purpose. The result is a gross sorting of marital life styles into Utilitarian and Intrinsic Marriages.

To say, or to observe, that someone is lastingly married is, we learned, more to announce an innocence than to describe a concrete reality. What kind of marriage is it, what purposes does it serve, and what other purposes are served tangentially and subordinately? Is his life mode chiefly the consequence of a conscious desire to fashion his existence in this way or is it the end product of a series of defaults, drifts, and residue from inattention and ineptness? Only the answers to such questions can dissolve the innocence.

The biological fact of heterosexuality is not so much a determining fact of life as a condition upon which different people build radically different life facts. The sexually expressive, the asexual, the apathetic, the hostile—all have built their characteristics upon the biological and cultural substructure of a two-sex order, but they have done it so differently that they are strangers to one another in this important regard, however close may be their affinities on political, recreational, or aesthetic matters.

At almost every point, the testimony of the 437 people has demonstrated the limited success of monolithic expectations in controlling their own or others' judgments and behavior. A large group, probably a majority, have borne children and reared them with responsibility and intelligence, but they have ignored the monogamous prescriptions about sex (especially premaritally). This majority holds the marriage bond to be inviolable, eschews any attempts to change spouses, yet at the same time often condones extramarital sexual relationships. Some do what they do quite openly; mostly they practice more or less effective concealment and observe various conventional pretenses. Much of this is typically the subject of an inordinate amount of gossip but is accompanied quite generally also by a pervasive tolerance which somewhat meliorates the censure.

Even where the judgment of conventional marital "success" must be rendered—as in the preponderant cases in which they marry once, remain married, rear children, and avoid any general public recognition of immorality—the success is often accomplished by following life styles of startlingly varied designs. Aside from the surface requirements, the conflict-habituated, the vital and the passive-congenial have practically nothing in common. Their daily routines, their sentiments, their aspirations, and practically everything about them are foreign to one another. Those in the Utilitarian Marriages and those in the Intrinsic Marriages are intellectual and emotional strangers to one another and, except insofar as a vague tolerance exists, tend to be proud of their separateness and disparaging of their manifestly different neighbors. Whatever way one wishes to formulate the questions about manners and morals, unequivocal answers are practically impossible.

What lies behind this vast amount of individuation which characterizes the marital and other sexual experience of these people? It has been brought about by a variety of causes, several of which are apparent in the material at hand, others only hinted. First of all, but not necessarily most important, are the roots in human protoplasm; a man or a woman is, before anything else, a biopsychic organism linked through heredity to an endless set of antecedent influences. The blind habits which are called culture, or education, or refinement do not always produce the results the mentors intend and individuals emerge willy-nilly from the efforts to standardize them by indoctrination. It is worth mentioning here that when David Riesman tried to explain the autonomous persons in *The Lonely Crowd,* he reached essentially the same conclusion—constitutionally they are different. He suggested that one could observe this in the nursery. And it doesn't yield to monolithic training as easily as desired, despite the impressive superstructure of church, school and informal pressure.

Despite the manifest conformist tendencies in today's

society, it is well not to overlook the abundance of opportunity for deviation which is also built into the social setting in which people grow up and function in their adult lives. While the mass media and large bureaucratic organizations like the church and education work in the direction of molding a common character type, these are counterbalanced by innumerable escape hatches for those who do not take to the standard curriculum. Easy mobility is one of these escapes. Deviation from expected behavior can be concealed by being performed at discreet distances from one's base of operations. If one gets caught he can simply move to another locale. He may often find a location in which customs considered deviant in the first community are quite acceptable in the new one. The anonymity which comes with metropolitan living is a further protection for individual expression. Travel is also a breeder of differences, particularly travel entailing substantial periods of residence in societies in which standards of conduct differ sharply from the Victorian-based standards professed where one was reared. The generation which we studied was profoundly influenced by periods of foreign military service for most of the men and some of the women. Many men pointed out to us, for example, that they trace their uneasiness with American women to their prolonged exposure to Japanese or French or German or Italian women and to the somewhat different sexual and marital standards which prevailed in these places. Higher education, particularly in the so-called liberal subjects—psychology, philosophy, anthropology—also provided a new perspective on the verbal provincialism within which most of the interviewees were reared. Anthropology illustrates and perhaps even dramatizes the relativity of moral standards; quite a few of the people we spoke to pointed out that their first real perspective on their own thoughtways and folkways came from their readings and discussions in anthropology concerning man and woman and moral conduct. All of these influences and perhaps others converge to have the seeming effect, whether or not so intended, of lending merit to ways of living that are clearly in contradiction to the traditional preachments.

Our findings probably apply also at levels of society other than the one we studied. The five relationship types are certainly not class bound. All five are well represented at all social levels, with the probable exception of the lowest strata, about which, in these terms, very little is known. We think it likely, however, that the proportions may be somewhat different at other class levels. A total relationship, for example, would be rather difficult for an assembly line worker —not impossible, but highly unlikely. On the other hand, for small, independent farmers it could easily be a more prevalent relationship than anywhere else in the social structure. The passive-congenial and the devitalized are probably to be found in every class, since they meet the general requirements of the monolithic code and at least approximate the kinds of fulfillments which by middle life large numbers of American people seem willing to settle for. Perhaps this is the reason why so much of the popular advice to the lovelorn and so many of the jokes and anecdotes about marriage seem to presuppose either a devitalized or a passive-congenial atmosphere.

Utilitarian Marriages, since they most perfectly encompass the passive-congenial and the devitalized relationships within the requirements of the monolithic code, probably express the world of man and woman for the clear majority of middle-aged couples, irrespective of education, income, religion, or other class-related differences. Yet everywhere there seems room for those couples who need and want Intrinsic Marriages and whose judgment and luck has found them suitable mates. Probably at different social levels the strains which threaten such a marriage are somewhat different, but not categorically so. A third party can destroy the cohesive unity of the intrinsically married in any class, but for a mechanic she probably wouldn't be the counterpart of the office wife any more than for the Significant American she is likely to be a waitress at the corner tavern.

Other involvements are also shaped by the differing conditions of class etiquette. Some of the forms we found among the Significant Americans are virtually impossible to maintain at other class levels, where an individual's work schedule and other comings and goings are subject to close scrutiny and to limitations imposed by modest amounts of money, brief vacations, and heavy family duties during leisure time. Even at the office party, which typically provides excellent opportunities for free-floating amour, the opportunities are different. The slightly tipsy stenographer dancing in her stockinged feet is not likely to appeal to the vice-president, but the third assistant to the buyer may find in her an invitation to adventure for the evening. A truck driver is not likely to be offered a call girl by the corporation he works for because he is expected to provide his own entertainment, yet as everyone knows, the call girl has counterparts at all social levels.

No one knows, except as inferences may be drawn from the Kinsey tables, how premarital and extramarital sexual activity and the grosser deviations may be distributed among the various social strata. Kinsey did show, for example, that completed premarital sex is more prevalent among the less educated, that sexual climax achieved by other than normal intercourse is more prevalent among the more educated, and that extramarital sexual outlets are more prevalent among the more educated. But these differences are not great and the Kinsey data are now almost twenty years old. More important, it seems to us, than technical statistical differences between social levels is the much more inclusive fact that at all social levels there are appreciable numbers of people whose conduct is not consistent with the expectations of the monolithic code, and that these people tend to find expression through various social customs which fit the circumstances of their own climate.

The so-called double standard of morality, which most observers seem to agree is less sharp than it once was, also appears importantly but variously at all social levels. It is probably the least distinct among the Significant Americans and for a number of reasons: the women, for example, have less need to fear pregnancy because they are obviously well and accurately informed concerning the physiology of reproduction, have access to the latest and best contraceptive methods, and find conditions for cohabitation which make it less difficult for them to put their knowledge to effective use. Perhaps even more important is the intellectual emancipation to which they have generally been exposed through their almost universal participation in higher education. Unlike the less educated, who tend to think of the double standard as inherent in nature, the well-educated man or woman sees the double standard in the light of the almost kaleidoscopic cultural variety of alternative sexual attitudes and practices.

But in all these respects the differences between the Upper Middle Class and the great majority of Americans, again, is not categorical. For example, people in the very numerous Lower Middle Class occupations are almost as well educated. Also, while their incomes are not as high, they are high enough to provide considerable latitude for recreation of many kinds. Some of their work schedules are also flexible and there is considerable mobility in their lives. Many of the work tasks throw men and women closely together in continuing and sometimes provocative ways. The difference, quite probably, is only one of degree—of the relative ease with which the Upper-Middle-Class man can express himself.

This would all seem to add up to an estimate that there are more similarities between middle-class people and the Significant Americans than there are differences. It is to be expected that what clear differences do occur are likely to be only those which are conditioned by grossly different circumstances and opportunities. For example, one cannot use a traveling job as an avoidance device unless he has the kind of job which enables him to travel, but he can use his activities as an itinerant weekend sportsman to accomplish a comparable goal. He cannot get involved with an office wife if he doesn't have one, but he can stop off for a drink every night with the unhappy wife in his car pool. And the woman at home can develop as much anxiety about the company picnic as the prominent person's wife about her husband's leisure activities while attending the London Conference. When the Significant American says he feels mismated, lonely, and isolated from his spouse, he may speak from the perspective of a different set of expectations, but loneliness between mates surely does not derive from class. And while there may be a difference between being a golf widow and a State Department widow, the fact of loneliness and the temptation to fill the gap may not be basically different.

So while we have tried in this report to stick to the facts and opinions of the people with whom we talked and to generalize only in terms of those findings, we have increasingly come to the conclusion that a study of other classes of American society would find that the problems, the successes, and the failures of the Significant Americans are not unique. The conditions of their private lives are more the outcroppings of their male and female natures, modified by variable life conditions and the complexities of modern society, than they are the inexorable consequences of being Significant Americans.

While our conversations with these people provided the substance of this inquiry, they also provided us with a jury to render judgment on the data. We encouraged our interviewees to discuss men and women in general as well as to present their own specific circumstances and feelings. Many of them, as the quotations have shown, did attempt the more encompassing task. They freely offered comparisons, critical judgments, estimates of the incidence of various deviations, linkages of cause and effect. One important dimension was their reaction to the larger picture, particularly where it suggested images which were unfamiliar or distasteful.

Three almost stereotyped reactions came up over and over again. First, there was the person with the "innocent" reaction. People who react this way live in a world of virtual make-believe. They pretend that men and women, of their social class at least, very rarely seek divorce, that statistical evidence of deviancy, however authentic, is grossly exaggerated, that Kinsey made up his statistics, and the premarital sex, at least for people known to them, is nil. They use a disarmingly naive test of what is true: what they personally see, at arm's length, is all there is to it. That the enormous amount of pretense, concealment, and etiquette seriously compromise the adequacy of such observation is not perceived. Yet they are anything but naive people in the other phases of their lives. As scientists, businessmen, diplomats, and soldiers they are trained realists, accustomed to handling evidence objectively. Still in this compartment of their thinking they cling almost childishly to an innocent interpretation and a narrowly local view of reality.

A second reaction type is the oversimplifier. His earmark is the single-cause explanation of any and everything about men and women. His favorite whipping boys are, as would be expected, higher education for women, out-of-home employment of women, decline of firm religious belief, drinking, uncensored literary expression, easy divorce laws, and poor parental example. As one of them said, all that is needed to solve our problems is "moral prophylaxis." It is not that the oversimplifier's reasoning is completely wrong—his error lies in his distortion; his myopic view of a complex situation fashions the mirage which he thinks is reality. He comes very close to "blaming people for the times they live in" or at least holding individuals accountable, somehow, for the pursuance of virtue, as if they lived in a vacuum instead of in a milieu and as if they functioned outside the laws of human psychology.

Well represented among the Significant Americans is a third group—the hard, even if also sometimes sad, realists. They see cause and effect as a complex, not in terms of one or a few selected simplitudes. And they see men and women as moved by outside forces as well as being self-directed forces themselves. They don't all go as far as the man who said, "We are free to do those things we must," but they do tend to have a healthy respect for the heavy impress of milieu and of psychology. These realists are found, of course, in all of the relationship types, in both sexes, in all occupations, and within both Utilitarian and Intrinsic Marriages. Some are personally conservative and some are avant garde, but mostly they are in the middle. Some feel that life has treated them rather well, others that their lot has been difficult, a few are embittered. But "We don't kid ourselves," said a young grandmother, "that the world is either prettier than it is or uglier than it is." They believe that people are to be held responsible for what they do, but only within the limits imposed by circumstances and by their own histories. They say that old rules can no longer be trusted, that traditional virtues can no longer be relied upon and new ones have not yet been proved. They realize that knowledge is rarely complete and yet that one must act here and now, with whatever perceptions and wisdom he can muster. And distortions are understood by them as an inherent part of perception and of reason. They are reluctant to insist that the content of their own consciences can or should be the measure of another's. That some of the oversimplifiers seem willing to so insist and that the innocents miss most of the real issues, should not be minimized. All three views are liberally scattered through the American populace and the voices of all are heard again and again in the endless dialogue about the intimate relationships of men and women.

As we listened to some of their descriptions of lost loves and thwarted hopes, we learned again that dispassionate objectivity is a most difficult obligation to carry off. Sorting through the records one final time, we are again reminded of the real people who provided them. An overriding compassion persists for those who played the game straight but were unable to keep up with and make adequate adjustment to relentless change. These people have lived long enough as a rule to have experienced important changes in themselves and in their spouses. Too often the forces within themselves and from the outside have required major reordering of self-concepts as well as of practical action. The person whose spouse moved away psychologically often committed no overt offense—yet his world of hope collapsed upon him. This is a hurtful thing to see; that one thinks he knows the reasons is small comfort; the fact won't go away.

Much the same for those who discovered themselves too late. Being honorable, or being trapped by the consequences of decisions made earlier, they often see no way, all things considered, ever to live their real selves. This kind of conjugal loneliness won't go away either, just because one now knows how he got there.

In other ways too, things don't work out in the man and woman world for so many—at least *they* don't think so. But they have to live with their own beliefs and feelings, not with those of someone from the objective outside.

One can only guess how much impact such knowings as

these have on the fashioning of the always present Utilitarian Marriage, the home base for the passive-congenial, the devitalized, the sexually apathetic and unfulfilled. It could hardly be other than a pressing influence.

Even if the Intrinsic Marriages decorate the brighter spot in the montage, the brightness is dimmed somewhat by the twin facts that they are a minority and that not all people capable and needful of vital relationship have found it possible to form and to hold on to one within the structure of monogamous marriage.

But perhaps this focus is all wrong. If majority opinion and action among the Significant Americans is accepted as a guide, the modest expectations and fulfillments of the Utilitarian Marriage are more in line with realism and with the total life commitments of the Significant Americans—and by implication, also for others differently situated. In this purview the Intrinsic Marriage is a minority arrangement by the middle years for the clear and sufficient reasons that it is not really suited to many and it doesn't fit smoothly with deeper commitments to the responsible goals of adult life.

*Some other Pelican books
are described on the
following pages*

Sexual Deviation
Anthony Storr

This book is a brief account of the common types of
sexual behaviour which are generally considered
perverse or deviant, together with explanations of
their origins.

Sado-masochism, fetishism, and other types of sexual
deviation are often assumed by the public to be the
result of satiety or else of inordinate desire. It is not
generally understood that the unhappy compulsions
which plague the deviant person are evidence of an
inability to achieve normal sexual relationships,
and that such people deserve compassion rather than
condemnation.

In this new Pelican Anthony Storr, the author of *The
Integrity of the Personality*, shows how sexual
deviations can result from inner feelings of sexual
guilt and inferiority which have persisted from
childhood. This is within everybody's understanding
It may seem a far cry from the lover's pinch to the
whip of the sado-masochist, but embryonic forms of
even the most bizarre deviations can be shown to
exist in all of us.

Everyone who is interested in sex – and which of us
is not – will be interested in this authoritative
account, not only because it explains the sexual
feelings of others, but also because it illuminates
some of their own.

Also available:

THE INTEGRITY OF THE PERSONALITY

Fundamentals of Psychology
C. J. Adcock

As publishers we recommend this new addition to the Pelican psychology series as a simple, logical, authoritative, and fair-minded introduction to psychology for all kinds of readers.

The author, who is a senior lecturer in New Zealand, has studied psychology both in England and in the United States. He approaches the study of human behaviour from the starting-point of our most primitive responses, the reflexes, which he explains simply in neurological terms. Illustrating his statements with concrete examples and with many instances from the most recent study of animal behaviour, he goes on to discuss our basic drives and needs, such as hunger, thirst, and the need for air, sleep, and security. His particular gift for advancing the reader's knowledge in easy stages allows him to explain the more complex workings of the autonomic nervous system and the processes of fear and anger, of learning, perception, and thinking, and of the patterning of personality in chapters which are as simple to comprehend as they are to read.

'Has succeeded in that most difficult task, the production of a good introductory text in psychology
– *The Times Educational Supplement*

Alcoholism

Niel Kessel and Henry Walton

Alcoholism is a serious illness. Physically it damages the body and shortens life. Socially it causes untold harm not only to the sufferer but also to his family.

Although middle-aged men are most affected, women alcoholics are increasing in number and young alcoholics are becoming numerous.

This book begins by considering what distinguishes the excessive from the social drinker. Physical, psychological and social factors all influence the development of the condition. What are alcoholics like and what are their chances of recovery? What part should the family and friends play, and the doctor and the hospitals? What can be learned from Alcoholics Anonymous?

Alcoholism is a fascinating study designed to explore, from the standpoint of the general reader, these aspects of an important social and medical problem.

The Psychology of Sex

Oswald Schwarz

As morality is the principle which governs and guards any human relationship, the main theme of this book is an analysis of the interaction of the physical sexual urge and the moral principle, with the conclusion that nothing that is truly natural can be really immoral. Such a statement makes sense only if morality is properly defined and clearly distinguished from what one may call conventional taboos. The much-discussed 'problem of sex' then stands revealed as the result of confusion of the real or essential morality with time-honoured but outworn convention.

On this basis the author analyses the various forms of sexual activity: masturbation, homosexuality in youth, prostitution, 'affairs'; and demonstrates that they are stages in a development which ultimately leads to marriage as the complete form of sexual relationship. A few case histories serve to illustrate the basic theory of this book and its application. The thesis that an 'essentially' moral sex life is the expression of the whole personality throws a light on, and provides a scientific basis for the discussion of, some social aspects of sex life, such as prostitution, birth control, and divorce.